In Search of the Blonde Tigress

ALSO BY SILVIA PETTEM

Separate Lives: The Story of Mary Rippon

Someone's Daughter: In Search of Justice for Jane Doe

Cold Case Research: Resources for Unidentified, Missing, and Cold Homicide Cases

The Long Term Missing: Hope and Help for Families

Cold Case Chronicles: Mysteries, Murders, and the Missing

IN SEARCH OF THE BLONDE TIGRESS

The Untold Story of Eleanor Jarman

SILVIA PETTEM

Essex, Connecticut

An imprint of Globe Pequot, the trade division of
The Rowman & Littlefield Publishing Group, Inc.
4501 Forbes Blvd., Ste. 200
Lanham, MD 20706
www.rowman.com

Distributed by NATIONAL BOOK NETWORK

British Library Cataloguing in Publication Information available

Library of Congress Cataloging-in-Publication Data
Names: Pettem, Silvia, author.
Title: In search of the Blonde Tigress : the untold story of Eleanor Jarman / Silvia Pettem.
Description: Essex, Connecticut : Lyons Press, [2023] | Includes bibliographical references and index.
Identifiers: LCCN 2022044308 (print) | LCCN 2022044309 (ebook) | ISBN 9781493068630 (cloth) | ISBN 9781493068647 (epub)
Subjects: LCSH: Jarman, Eleanor, 1901- | Female offenders--United States. | Fugitives from justice--United States.
Classification: LCC HV6046 .P47 2023 (print) | LCC HV6046 (ebook) | DDC 364.3/74--dc23/eng/20221024
LC record available at https://lccn.loc.gov/2022044308
LC ebook record available at https://lccn.loc.gov/2022044309

∞™ The paper used in this publication meets the minimum requirements of American National Standard for Information Sciences—Permanence of Paper for Printed Library Materials, ANSI/NISO Z39.48-1992.

This book is dedicated to Eleanor's ten grandchildren. Their lives overlapped with Eleanor's, but they never got to meet her.

Contents

ILLUSTRATIONS

Characters

Anderson, George: One of George Dale's two aliases

Avery, Dr. Elmer K.: Physician for Eleanor Jarman's boys; wrote letter of support

Batara, Thomas: Screen name for Richard Slater in *Gang Busters* television show

Berendt, Amelia: Mother of Eleanor Jarman

Berendt, Dorothy Burger: Wife of Otto Berendt

Berendt, Ella Marie: Eleanor Jarman's childhood name

Berendt, Hattie: One of Eleanor Jarman's sisters; cared for her boys

Berendt, Julius: Father of Eleanor Jarman

Berendt, Otto: One of Eleanor Jarman's brothers

Burrus, Elsie: Co-worker of Eleanor; wrote letter of support

Cox, Mrs. Ollie: Mother of Lula Herzfeld/Herzfield; wrote letter of support

Dale, George (aka George Anderson/Kennedy): Convicted in the murder of Gustav Hoeh

Dale, John M.: Father of George Dale

DeOliveira, Pat: One of LaVerne Francis Jarman's daughters

Ferlic, Frank J.: Second defense attorney for George Dale

Foster, Mary: Alias for Margaret Keringer at time of escape with
Eleanor Jarman

Glass, Albert: Arresting officer of Eleanor Jarman and George Dale

Goldschmidt, Darrell: Stepson of Hermina Herzfeld/Herzfield
Goldschmidt; wrote letter of support

Goldschmidt, Hermina Herzfeld/Herzfield: Sister of Richard
Slater; wrote letter of support

Hazard, Helen H.: Superintendent of Oakdale Reformatory

Herzfeld/Herzfield, Lula: Sister-in-law of Richard Slater; wrote
letter of support

Herzfeld/Herzfield, Nathan: Birth name of Richard Slater

Hoeh, Carrie: Wife of Gustav Hoeh

Hoeh, Earl: One of Gustav Hoeh's two sons

Hoeh, Gustav: Shopkeeper, murder victim

Hoeh, Norman: One of Gustav Hoeh's two sons

Hull, Margaret Dale: Sister of George Dale; claimed George's body

Jarman, Daniel: Older son of Ruby and LeRoy Michael Jarman

Jarman, Douglas: Younger son of Ruby and LeRoy Michael Jarman

Jarman, Eleanor: Convicted as accomplice in murder of Gustav Hoeh

Jarman, LaVerne Francis: Younger son of Eleanor and Michael Roy
Jarman

Jarman, LeRoy Michael: Older son of Eleanor and Michael Roy
Jarman

Jarman, Michael Roy: Husband of Eleanor Jarman

Jarman, Ruby Golden: Wife of LeRoy Michael Jarman

Kennedy, George: One of George Dale's two aliases

Keringer, Margaret: Eleanor's escape partner (under alias of Mary Foster)

Lahey, Ed: Newspaper columnist who wrote on Eleanor

Makaron/Mackeron, Margaret: Married name of Margaret Keringer, Eleanor's escape partner

Malone, Captain Willard L.: Chicago Police Department, Austin Police Station

Miller, Joe: Alias for Leo Minneci

Millman, Marie H.: Likely alias for Eleanor Jarman

Minneci, Emil: Brother of Leo Minneci; owner of getaway car

Minneci, Leo (aka Joe Miller): Convicted as accomplice in murder of Gustav Hoeh

Minneci, Tina: Wife of Leo Minneci

Oliver, Sandra: Step-granddaughter of Richard Slater

Power, Joseph P.: First defense attorney for George Dale

Schultze, A. Jefferson: Defense attorney for Eleanor Jarman

Slater, Beaulah Nell Thompson: Wife of Richard Slater

Slater, Richard ("Dick"): "Very close friend" of Eleanor Jarman

Swoik, James: One of the "daylight" robbery victims; rebuttal witness

Zuta, Jack: Chicago gangster

Foreword

They rank as some of the most notorious female criminals in the history of the United States. Bonnie Parker shot up the American South and Midwest as the partner to Clyde Barrow. Kate "Ma" Barker plagued the country as the matriarch of her gang of relatives. Patty Hearst, though eventually pardoned, enthralled and repulsed the nation as a gun-toting member of the Symbionese Liberation Army.

What about Eleanor Jarman?

In the mid-1930s, the same gangster era that included Bonnie and Clyde, the Barker-Karpis Gang, Baby Face Nelson, and Machine Gun Kelly, Eleanor Jarman became as infamous as any other bank robber or killer in the United States—man or woman.

Jarman even had a nickname. "The blonde tigress," the rabid press in her adopted city of Chicago dubbed her. But Jarman did not rob banks. She did not kill anyone. She wasn't a gun moll—a woman whose main role was to look glamorous on the arm of her lawbreaking boyfriend.

Eleanor Jarman got caught up in violence—a fatal holdup. She was convicted. She was sentenced to an astounding 199 years. But Jarman made a name for herself primarily as an escapee. When she died, most likely in 1980, she was a record-setting fugitive. She was never caught and is believed to have been on the lam longer than any female convict in the United States.

How Jarman broke out of prison is not a mystery. Neither is why she opted for an endless life on the run. What remains uncertain is the level of her involvement in the crime that led to her incarceration, as well as what kind of help she had in managing to stay so many steps ahead of the law for so long. Also mysterious is the name Jarman adopted as a fugitive and what jobs she held as she carved out a new identity for herself, all the while facing the possibility that she would be found out, captured, and sent back to prison.

Silvia Pettem takes on these mysteries. In her comprehensive study of Eleanor Jarman, Pettem pieces together clues to make a convincing case for what Jarman was doing in her later years. Equally fascinating is Pettem's examination of Jarman's life before she became a fugitive—a life in which Jarman achieved a degree of independence and self-reliance that would have made her stand out for her time even if she had never garnered unwanted celebrity as a criminal.

Jarman never gave up. She overcame, often on her own, the two most powerful forces during the 1930s: the Great Depression and the federal government's war on gangsters, bank robbers, and other crooks who thrived during and after Prohibition.

And, of course, Jarman was a woman. She challenged the male-dominated culture as a regular citizen and as an outlaw. Perhaps that is the primary reason she captured the imagination of so many newspaper reporters and commentators. Perhaps that is why the press, in addition to calling her "the blonde tigress," also labeled her "the most dangerous woman alive." As a woman, Eleanor Jarman was a different kind of public enemy, but—in the view of the powerful—she was a public enemy nonetheless.

Jarman's journey to the wanted list features many characters. The crime she was convicted of committing included a victim and a lifetime of grief for his family. In turning into a fugitive, Jarman gained freedom for herself but denied justice for those she and her fellow defendants were found guilty of harming. That cannot be forgotten.

But did Jarman deserve her fate? Did she get a fair trial? Was her 199-year sentence reasonable?

While Silvia Pettem offers solutions to many of the mysteries surrounding Eleanor Jarman, some questions might always be left unanswered. Jarman—though her position among notorious American female criminals is now secure—might be destined to stay elusive. She might be destined to remain forever on the run.

Jerry Clark, PhD, FBI Special Agent (Retired)

Ed Palattella, award-winning investigative crime reporter

Authors of *On the Lam: A History of Hunting Fugitives in America*

INTRODUCTION

In 1933, a thirty-two-year-old mother of two was sensationalized by newspaper reporters as the "blonde tigress." Her name was Eleanor Jarman. Although the press made her out to be a vicious criminal, a closer look at her life reveals an otherwise ordinary woman who got caught up in a Chicago crime spree, then was convicted as an accomplice to murder and sent to prison for 199 years. Yet, after serving only seven years, she escaped.

It's easy to imagine Eleanor, in her later years and in her waitress uniform, confiding in close friends, but would they have believed her? She took up her life where she left off and, for forty years, hid in plain sight. That's what makes her story so compelling, and speculation on her life on the lam was the challenge that hooked me into trying to find her.

Researching and writing about historical characters requires figurative trips back in time to dig into the past. Fortunately for me, I had two highly skilled researchers to share my journey. The three of us—each on our own computers and in different parts of the country—searched and slogged our way through every minute detail of Eleanor's life, solving some mysteries and unearthing others. We shared several theories and made a good team, as we approached the research from different angles and often with different databases.

In Search of the Blonde Tigress: The Untold Story of Eleanor Jarman started out as a biography, but once we peeled back the layers of Eleanor's life, we found pieces of a detective story that only needed to be assembled. Partway through the process, I brought in a family member of Eleanor's escape partner, as well as the step-granddaughter of the man who came to be known as Eleanor's "very close friend."

Throughout our investigation, my colleagues and I remained energized, and the hunt kept us going. There's a sadness in realizing that the bulk of our research on Eleanor is done, but we will continue to pursue new tangents to see where they may lead. What follows is our best-case scenario.

Silvia Pettem

Part I

Hardships and Temptations

CHAPTER 1

Polka-Dotted Dress

THURSDAY, AUGUST 8, 1940, STARTED OUT LIKE ANY OTHER DAY AT THE Oakdale Reformatory for Women near the small town of Dwight, in rural Illinois. Helen H. Hazard, the institution's prim forty-four-year-old superintendent, sat at her desk in the administration building going over staff reports, but her eyes wandered toward her office window. She stopped shuffling papers for a moment and reflected on the ten years she'd held the job, ever since Illinois's only correctional facility solely for women opened in 1930. Miss Hazard, as she was called, knew every "girl" by name and ran a tight ship. Her staff tracked and supervised every step of each of the inmates as they followed their daily work schedules. Everything, and everyone, moved about with flawless precision, or so she thought.

Except for steel bars on the windows, the "cottage-type" institution resembled a country estate, and the Tudor-style prison facility was anything but imposing. Only a sign and a twelve-foot wire fence topped with barbed wire separated the 260 inmates from the surrounding corn fields and the outside world. Most of the women accepted their lot in life and bided their time until their sentences were up.

But on this muggy summer day, after a lunchtime head count, word quickly reached the superintendent's office that two women were missing. Staff members, prison officials, and even Superintendent Hazard herself immediately searched the premises.

Inmates Eleanor Jarman and Margaret Keringer (under the alias of "Mary Foster") had last been seen at 11 a.m. when they were at their

3

assigned jobs cleaning the staff's quarters. Both women were slender and petite with pulled-back shoulder-length hair, and they were close in age. Eleanor, at thirty-nine, was the more attractive of the two, but her crooked front teeth showed prominently when she smiled. Margaret looked older than her thirty-eight years and somewhat haggard. She spoke with a distinct foreign accent that kept her from concealing her Hungarian origin.

For the seven years since her incarceration in 1933, Eleanor had kept to herself. Margaret, however, had racked up multiple arrests and confinements in other states and was admitted to the Oakdale Reformatory in 1939. Superintendent Hazard and her staff were unaware that the two women were acquaintances or possibly even friends. Both inmates, however, had "rooms" near each other on the second floor of one of the cell blocks. A newspaper writer later conveyed that Margaret had asked to be moved closer to Eleanor's cell, but that prison officials had denied the request. Did Margaret, a hardened and habitual criminal who already had escaped from two other prisons, conceive of an escape plan and see an advantage in bringing Eleanor along?

Perhaps the women communicated through other inmates, as all of the women were allowed five minutes to visit with each other before each meal. Eleanor and Margaret may have devised an escape plan during one of those times or on previous shared work assignments. First, though, they had to go about their normal routines, then wait for an opportune moment to put their plan into action. It came when they were on housework duty and a staff member was distracted. Details are sketchy, but at some point Margaret "fixed a safety catch" on a normally locked heavy steel door. The two women also entered a closet used by the staff and stole a blue skirt and matching blue jacket, as well as a polka-dotted dress.

As Superintendent Hazard later pieced together the escape for the press, Eleanor and Margaret fled to the northeast portion of the prison complex, where they hid behind a long brick laundry building that was located on the edge of the prison grounds. The women weren't seen, as no laundry was being done that day and the unoccupied structure concealed their view from the rest of the prison complex. With only the stolen street clothes concealed on their bodies, Eleanor and Margaret managed to climb the wire fence and get over the barbed wire before lowering themselves down the other side. There, they quickly changed clothes and tucked their prison garb into a clump of bushes.

With one of the women wearing the blue suit and the other the polka-dotted dress, the fleeing felons darted through acres of soon-to-be-harvested fields of corn. It was August, and, by then, the stalks had grown so high that they shielded the women from all directions. As soon as Superintendent Hazard confirmed that Eleanor and Margaret were no longer on the prison grounds, she summoned guards from the Pontiac Reformatory and the Statesville Prison to aid the Illinois State Police in a search that even included a small plane to view the fields from above. The guards and police also set up roadblocks in all directions. Surely, they thought, the women would be apprehended before they got far, but the combined forces' hastily arranged procedures came too late. Eleanor and Margaret already had managed to slip away.

All police officers, down to local patrolmen, were told to "be on the lookout" for Eleanor and Margaret. Residents of nearby farms looked out, too, and locked their doors. As they huddled around their console radios for updates, they heard report after report of Eleanor, the "notorious murderess," and her "companion." A few hours later, an insurance agent came forward to explain that he had given two women a ride toward the town of Morris (nineteen miles north of the reformatory), but he had dropped them off part way when he turned off the highway to his home. When Superintendent Hazard showed him photos of Eleanor and Margaret, he quickly identified them. The women, the insurance agent said, told him that they had come from the town of Streator, Illinois, and were headed to Chicago. One of them wore a polka-dotted dress.

After Eleanor and Mary got out of the man's car, a farmer gave the women a ride the rest of the way into Morris. There, a rural mail carrier reported seeing them, as described, on the northern outskirts of town. A gasoline station attendant reported that they had stopped at his station, indicating their intentions to hitch a ride toward Chicago. Likely they reached the big city, where someone must have at least given them a meal and a change of clothing.

Back at the reformatory, staff members reported the thefts of the skirt, jacket, and polka-dotted dress. Superintendent Hazard, meanwhile, questioned and then suspended the staff member who had been trusted with their care. When the superintendent was asked about the escaped women, she told the press that Eleanor "had been a model prisoner and never before had made trouble." Of Margaret's behavior, the superintendent replied, "Not quite so good." Margaret, in fact, had a long rap sheet for grand larceny and bank robbery, so it made sense that she was the instigator and took Eleanor along.

The press and, thus, the public interpreted the situation differently. Eleanor had been convicted in 1933 as an accomplice to murder after participating in a series of "daylight robberies" with two men on Chicago's west side. One of the men was her "sweetheart" George Dale who fired the fatal shot at an elderly shop owner. Reporters were quick to dub Eleanor the "blonde tigress," after they falsely claimed that Eleanor had clawed at and kicked the victim as he lay dying on the sidewalk. At the time of her and Margaret's escape, reporters all over the country wrote about the "Tiger girl and her pal." No one in the press bothered to debate as to whether Eleanor had been guilty as charged or if her role in the crime been exaggerated.

Eleanor, in even more sensationalized news reports, became known as "the most dangerous woman alive." Perhaps Margaret had picked Eleanor solely for her notoriety, in hopes that the police would search harder for the "tigress" than for her. If this was Margaret's strategy, it did not end as planned.

CHAPTER 2

The Tenth Child

NOTHING HAD BEEN NOTORIOUS OR EVEN OUT OF THE ORDINARY ABOUT Eleanor's growing-up years. Born and raised in Sioux City, Iowa, she toed the line as the tenth child in a poor working-class family. Only after she married and had children, then moved to Chicago and lived on her own, did she enter the world of crime.

SIOUX CITY, IOWA, 1901

Eleanor came into the world as Ella Marie Berendt, on April 22, 1901—a spring day that the *Sioux City Journal* noted had "an almost cloudless sky." Purple lilacs broke the bleakness of winter, their scent filtering through the open screen door of the Berendt family's small, rented house. For Eleanor's mother, Amelia, however, there was no time to appreciate the coming of spring, nor to rejoice in the slight breeze that blew the smells of the nearby stockyards in the opposite direction. The thirty-seven-year-old wife and mother, swollen and ripe with pregnancy, maneuvered her way down the back steps to the clothesline to take down the diapers—the same ones she'd soaked in the wash tub, then scrubbed on a washboard and hung out to dry for child after child.

Amelia's labor pains increased in intensity, but she couldn't rest. In addition to the never-ending laundry, she had nine mouths to fill, including herself and her husband Julius. The couple's oldest son Paul, age thirteen, was in school, but any minute he'd run through the front door, followed by Henry, Hattie, Otto, and the twins, Frieda and Alfred.

Each demanded Amelia's attention while Frank, a typical two year old, no longer was willing to take a nap.

Their father, Julius, known for his big red beard, was temporarily unemployed from his work as a laborer at the Cudahy meat-packing plant. But he recently had taken on a new job as janitor for the St. Paul's Evangelical German Lutheran Church where the whole family could be found on Sundays. Amelia, no doubt, wanted him home, but her thoughts quickly turned to the new baby. Would this child survive? And what would be his or her fate in life?

With support from the neighborhood midwife, Amelia focused on giving birth, and the noise of her other children faded into the background. Soon, Eleanor's cry let everyone know that another child had joined the family. Amelia thought back to a son who was stillborn and to another who died as an infant. This child was her tenth. With little Eleanor the newest member of the family, life in the Berendt household settled into a familiar routine. Julius came home from work, split wood for the stove, and helped the older children with their schoolwork. Life went on.

AN UNMARKED GRAVE

Amelia had no way of knowing that her drained and weary body would carry and bear two more children—Charlotte, who would die young, and then John, who would live to old age. But Amelia never quite recovered from John's birth. On Tuesday July 16, 1907, when John was only six months old, Amelia lay down on her bed and didn't get back up. She passed away at the age of forty-three.

Two days later, all nine surviving children, along with their father Julius, quietly watched as Amelia's casket was lowered into the ground in Sioux City's Floyd Cemetery. The Lutheran pastor said a few comforting words, likely in German. And for the first time that anyone could remember, the children's voices were hushed. A laborer from the cemetery filled the grave with dirt, but the site was left unmarked as Julius couldn't afford a stone. At the time, Eleanor, then second youngest of the surviving children, was six years old. Dr. John Hermann told her that her mama had gone to heaven because of a problem with her heart, but Eleanor, no doubt, knew that Amelia died because she worked too hard.

GERMAN HERITAGE

Julius and Amelia had left their homeland for America in 1886, but they didn't make their long ship voyages together. Julius (and likely Amelia, as well) came from West Prussia, then part of the German Empire. Amelia followed Julius two months later. The two were part of a massive migration of German-speaking immigrants who set off to start new lives in a new land. Full of hopes and expectations, the young people said goodbye to friends and family but brought their language and religion with them. Most of these German-speaking immigrants settled in the upper Midwest, attracted by the vast expanse of land available to home-steaders. In Iowa, they turned over the prairie sod and planted crops. Many of the farmers raised corn that was fed to cattle and hogs. The resulting stock-raising industry led to Sioux City's stockyards, where Julius found work.

Amelia probably didn't have much room in her traveling bag, but perhaps she tucked in a small remembrance of her homeland, such as an embroidered handkerchief, a pin or brooch, or a handmade lace collar or shawl. If so, it may have added a special touch to her best dress as she and Julius stood side by side on February 18, 1887, to recite their marriage vows. Years later, when Eleanor was a very young girl playing "dress up," as many girls do, perhaps Amelia showed the fancy item or items to her daughter, giving her an appreciation for more than her usual hand-me-down clothes.

COMING OF AGE IN SIOUX CITY

Amelia's death, in 1907, made life even more difficult for the suddenly motherless family. The older siblings also found work in the meat-packing plants. Sisters Hattie and Frieda dropped out of school to help raise their younger siblings, including Eleanor and baby John. Eleanor left school after the sixth or seventh grade. Then, according to information she would provide to reformatory officials many years later, she worked as a waitress "irregularly since 12 years of age." By 1915, she was living with her sister Hattie who then was twenty-four years old and the only sibling, at the time, who had married. Eleanor likely helped Hattie and her husband with their three children. Members of the family looked out for each other.

Hattie's husband worked in the stockyards. In addition to pens packed with cattle and hogs, it held sheep, horses, and mules and contained loading docks, scales, business offices, a bank, and more than one restaurant. Years later, a newspaper story on Eleanor mentioned that she had, at one time, worked in one of the stockyards' restaurants as a waitress—the one occupation she would return to again and again in her life. Perhaps over scrambled eggs or a cup of coffee, Eleanor met Michael Roy Jarman, her future husband.

Looming overseas, at the time, was the Great War, now referred to as World War I. Michael Roy signed up for the draft, stating on his registration form that he was twenty-one years old, of medium height and build, with blue eyes and light brown hair. He worked as a laborer in the stockyards and supported his father, mother, and a sister. Even so, he was drafted into the Army. As Private First Class in the 20th Infantry, he was sent to Vladivostok, Siberia. When he returned, Michael Roy would become Eleanor's ticket out of town.

"LITTLE CHICAGO"

Michael Roy's family, also a large one, had moved to Sioux City in 1916, from Neligh, Nebraska. The Jarmans were Catholic, and Michael Roy was the sixth of twelve children. Their parents were native born, but one set of grandparents had immigrated from Ireland and the other from Wales. Although crime had not infiltrated Eleanor's family, it did impact the Jarman household. Of the six sons in the family, only one, John, didn't have any publicized run-ins with the law.

Eleanor's father, Julius, died in January 1920 when Eleanor was eighteen years old. Again, she and her siblings, most of whom still lived in Sioux City, watched as a beloved parent was lowered into the ground. That same year, Eleanor and her husband-to-be traveled to Lincoln, Nebraska, where their names were recorded under "Marriage Licenses" in the *Lincoln Star*. Eleanor still used her birth name of "Ella M." for

Ella Marie. By September 1921, the young couple temporarily returned to Sioux City, where Eleanor gave birth to the couple's first son, LeRoy Michael. They returned, again, prior to October 1923 for the birth of their second son, LaVerne Francis.

The year of the Jarmans' marriage also was the first year of national prohibition. The Eighteenth Amendment to the US Constitution went into effect in 1920 and outlawed the manufacture, sale, and transportation of intoxicating liquors. Even so, there continued to be a big demand for the consumption of beer, wine, and liquor, and that demand created a market for the illegal manufacture and sale of alcoholic beverages. At least two of Michael Roy's brothers jumped on the supply train. One was James, who was set free from an accomplice-to-murder charge after serving only eight years of a twenty-five-year sentence. He then made moonshine, sold some to a federal agent, and was arrested again. Because of the city's activity in marketing these products, Sioux City gained its nickname, "Little Chicago."

Probably in 1925, Michael Roy, already a heavy drinker, was ready for a move into the heart of the action. Eleanor may have been a willing partner at the time, or perhaps she just followed her husband. Either way, Eleanor, Michael Roy, LeRoy, and LaVerne left Sioux City and moved to the big city of Chicago, without any idea of what it would offer.

THE BIG CITY

Whether the downward spiral of Eleanor and Michael Roy's marriage had to do with alcohol is not known, but it likely was a contributing factor. Years later, in an interview with a reporter from *The Lincoln Star*, Eleanor referred to her husband as "a worthless lout," stating that she had tolerated his habitual drunkenness until one night when he tried to take the children with him to a saloon. The boys had been quarantined for whooping cough and were only two and four years old. Chicago police then arrested Michael Roy for nonsupport, and he served a nine-month sentence in the Cook County Jail. Somehow, Eleanor managed to move, with her sons LeRoy and LaVerne, to an apartment of her own. She must have saved up every penny, gone on relief, or had a friend, or friends, to help her.

By the late 1920s, Eleanor and the boys had settled into a fifty-five-dollar-per-month apartment in the Garfield Terrace Building, a large apartment complex at 3459 West Madison Street. The building is no longer standing, but it was located at the intersection of West Madison Street and South St. Louis Avenue in the West Chicago neighborhood of East Garfield Park. West Madison was, and is, a major east-west thoroughfare, north of and roughly paralleling today's Interstate 280 and heading east to the downtown area known as "the Loop."

Straight west on West Madison Street was what was called the Madison-Crawford District, a thriving "city within a city" built on the site of a former racetrack for horses. A 1931 *Chicago Tribune* reporter stated that the area, a product of modern times, had become citified "as if touched by a magic wand," adding that it "leaped from babyhood, through adolescence, and into sophisticated maturity overnight." A highlight was the "glittering" Paradise Theater. The district still retained two police officers to direct traffic, but the suburban community was the first in Chicago to install "stop-and-go" traffic signals. Automobiles mixed with streetcars, the city was thriving, and people were always on the move.

The newspaper reporter added that the district also was fortunate to have "the green foliage of Garfield Park at its doors." Eleanor's apartment, adjoining the park, was a good location, especially for LeRoy and LaVerne. There, on 172 acres, expansive green lawns between tree-lined streets provided a breath of fresh air in the middle of the bustling city. No doubt the boys, like most little boys, played in the park's lagoons. Sioux City had become a distant memory.

If the family had a radio, all three may have avidly listened to multiple episodes of "Amos 'n' Andy," a radio sitcom that had its first broadcasts, from Chicago, in 1928. The nightly comedies featured characters Amos Jones and Andy Brown, two men who left their farm in Atlanta, Georgia, and moved to Chicago, where they started a taxi service. Their adventures and mishaps in a setting close to home would have kept the boys and Eleanor entertained.

The Garfield Terrace apartment building also was close to Thompson's Restaurant, only two blocks to the east on West Madison Street at

Figure 2.1. Eleanor's apartment was adjacent to Garfield Park. Originally named Central Park, it was renamed in 1881 for President James Garfield after his assassination. Library of Congress, public domain.

its intersection with South Kedzie Avenue. A few years later, in court testimony, Eleanor would state that she worked, presumably at Thompson's, for three or more years as a waitress. In the 1920s, Chicago had forty-nine of these cafeteria-style restaurants. Ahead of their times, the Thompson chain offered "fast food," with sandwiches that included cervelat sausage (similar to salami), smoked boiled tongue, cold boiled ham, hot frankfurters, cold corned beef, cold salmon, and Herkimer County cheese, all served on "Milwaukee Rye Bread" baked by the restaurant chain's own bakery.

Either in Thompson's or in one of the other restaurants where Eleanor was employed, she struck up a friendship with coworker Elsie Burrus who, in 1935, would write a letter on Eleanor's behalf to accompany her application for clemency from the Oakdale Reformatory. Elsie would describe Eleanor as a hard worker, a trusted employee, and a kind mother to her two children. Perhaps the women traded daycare, working around school schedules. Also on West Madison Street, three blocks to the east from Eleanor's apartment, was the office of Dr. Elmer K. Avery.

Like Elsie, Dr. Avery also was a friend who, one day, would stand up for Eleanor's character, stating that she was well liked and steady at her work and that her boys always were mannerly and well behaved.

Although Eleanor and her husband Michael Roy clearly had separated, there is no record of a divorce. Even if there wasn't one, the legality of the couple's marriage didn't keep Michael Roy from remarrying or Eleanor, at some point, from seeking male companionship. Likely she relied on her women friends for advice on avoiding another pregnancy, but if she got up the nerve to talk about the almost taboo topic of birth control with Dr. Avery, he may have told her about sponges and condoms.

At least part of the time that Eleanor and the boys lived in the Garfield Terrace Building, Eleanor had a live-in boyfriend. He was mentioned a few years later in a newspaper story, but his name was not revealed by the press. Exactly when they lived together is not known, but further research has shown that, in 1930, the man had an apartment on North Hamlin Avenue, on the west side of Garfield Park. Then, during 1931 and 1932, he maintained an address on South St. Louis Avenue, just around the corner from the Garfield Terrace Building.

During a lull in Eleanor's work as a waitress, she worked part time for her boyfriend, answering the telephone for a business that he ran out of yet another apartment—within a block of Thompson's Restaurant. Later documents reveal that Eleanor had been, for five or six years, well acquainted with his siblings and their families. In court testimony, Eleanor would call him her "friend," and she would turn to him in time of need—even after she moved on to George Dale, her well-publicized "sweetheart" and partner in crime.

CHAPTER 3

Crimes

GEORGE DALE WAS A FACTORY WORKER IN CHICAGO'S FAR NORTH SIDE. There, at 1054 Leland Avenue, he shared an apartment with his older sister Margaret Dale Hull. She, like Eleanor, also was a waitress with two children, but they were not living with her at the time. Margaret had been forced to send them to the "Chicago Nursery and Half-Orphan Asylum," described as "a home for children of single-parent families in dire financial straits." The stock market crash during the previous year of 1929 was followed by a severe economic turndown that affected all classes of society. Particularly hard hit were single parents.

GEORGE

George, his sister Margaret, and their siblings had grown up in Fredericktown, Missouri, a small lead-mining community surrounded by forests ninety miles south of St. Louis, Missouri. George was described in his hometown newspaper as "a well-liked and well-behaved youth." He played on his high school's football team and was listed among the seniors in his class who had "perfect answers in the sermon contest." At the time of the 1930 federal census, George's father, John Dale, was a seventy-one-year-old widowed grocer who still resided in Fredericktown, where he lived with his youngest daughter.

According to testimony that Eleanor later would give in court, she and George met in the winter of 1932–1933. By then, he had grown tired of working on the assembly line at the Stewart Warner radio factory. After watching his sister struggle through the death of her husband and the temporary absence of her children, George may have weighed his choices and decided to find another way to make a living.

By 1933, what is now called the Great Depression had reached its lowest point with an estimated fifteen million unemployed Americans. Meanwhile, nearly half of the country's banks had failed. Except for Eleanor's part-time job answering telephones, even she was out of work. Later she would testify that before meeting George, she had accepted "relief" from a private charity. Then, perhaps over a beer, George stepped in and helped with rent, groceries, and clothing for the children. Life for the four of them became easier—for a while.

SERVING BEER

Although Eleanor's former boyfriend still lingered in the background, George swept her off her feet. George also had additional aliases including George Kennedy and George Anderson. Eleanor probably didn't ask any questions. Early in 1933, Eleanor, LeRoy, and LaVerne moved in with George at 4300 West Madison Street, a short streetcar ride from the Garfield Terrace apartment. A pharmacy and other retail businesses took up the first floor of the building, with apartments on the second and third floors. In a later court hearing, a judge would refer to Eleanor and George's apartment as "a den of iniquity." Other references even mentioned wild parties. In actuality, the apartment may have doubled as a "beer flat."

National Prohibition had been in effect for thirteen long years. Illicit bars, called "speakeasies," required passwords to enter. As the liquor flowed, small jazz bands played tunes made popular by Duke Ellington and Louis Armstrong. Also popular, especially in midwestern cities, were "flats" (apartments) that served beer. An estimated five thousand of these more informal family businesses thrived in Chicago alone. Wherever one lived in the city, stated a newspaper reporter at the time, there likely was a "beer flat" next door or across the street. The proprietor may or may not have been employed elsewhere during the day, but he kept a barrel of beer on ice in his apartment's kitchen. Then he simply set up bridge tables in his living or dining room and welcomed his friends and neighbors.

In later court testimony, Eleanor would state that she had worked in a "beer flat" until legalized beer put it out of business. If she was referring to the 4300 West Madison apartment, George likely was the proprietor. If so, Eleanor, as the waitress, served her customers with mugs of the homebrew for twenty-five cents apiece, just as actress Barbara Stanwyk did in the 1933 film *Baby Face*. The newspaper writer reported that raids were infrequent, as Prohibition enforcement officers were too busy shutting off the beer at the source—from the big syndicates. Still, the operations in private residences were illegal. Perhaps LeRoy and LaVerne helped serve as well. If so, Eleanor may have rationalized that she was sparing her boys from being sent to the children's home, as George's sister had been forced to do with her children.

The end of "beer flats" in Chicago and in other towns and cities across the country came on March 22, 1933, when the nation's new president, Franklin D. Roosevelt, signed the Beer and Wine Revenue Act legalizing the sale of 3.2 percent beer. Even though this lower-alcohol beer was less intoxicating than the homemade varieties, "beer flat" patrons took their business elsewhere. December 1933 would bring an end to national pro-hibition and legalize regular beer, wine, and liquor. But by then Eleanor no longer would be serving beer. Instead she would be serving time. It's more than a coincidence that the final days of Eleanor's participation in the beer business coincided with her imminent involvement in more serious crime.

CONTEMPORARIES

Out of work and during the worst of the Depression era, Eleanor, now living with George, had more time to read the newspapers and listen to the radio. Although Eleanor's years on her own had overlapped gang-ster Al Capone's struggles to control Chicago's organized crime, the real-time exploits of Depression-era contemporaries Bonnie Parker and Clyde Barrow were more likely to have caught Eleanor's attention. These young and attractive crime partners robbed banks, grocery stores, and gas stations throughout the Midwest, while murdering anyone who got in their way.

Figure 3.1. In December 1933, these patrons of a Chicago bar celebrated the repeal of National Prohibition. DN-A-4954, Chicago Sun-Times/Chicago Daily News collection, Chicago History Museum.

The allure of Bonnie and Clyde was due, in part, to a roll of undeveloped film that police seized in a raid in April 1933. The police then developed the photos, showing the nattily dressed couple posed with their automobile and their weapons. Instead of worrying about being caught, they seemed to almost encourage the police to come and find them. The press practically elevated the two to the status of folk heroes and splashed their photos across the front pages of newspapers all over the country.

Also capturing the public's attention at the time was Robert Elliott Burns. Bonnie and Clyde had not yet been caught, but Burns was an escaped convict. In 1921, the World War I veteran was involved in a minor robbery of less than five dollars in the state of Georgia. He then suffered harsh treatment when he was sentenced to at least six years of hard labor on a prison chain gang. He escaped and fled to Chicago, where he lived under an assumed name. Without being recognized, he became a well-respected and successful magazine publisher. He married, but his wife turned him in after he admitted his love for another woman. He ended up back on the chain gang, but he escaped a second time to live and work in Newark, New Jersey.

There, he authored *I Am a Fugitive from a Georgia Chain Gang!*, originally published in 1931 in serialized editions of *True Detective* magazine. In November 1932, Warner Brothers released, under a slightly different name, *I Am a Fugitive from a Chain Gang*, a gripping crime-drama film based on Burns's book. Again, assuming an alias, Burns went to Hollywood and assisted in the film's direction. The film was a big hit and played in major theaters all over the country. Only a couple of weeks after its release, Burns openly gave a newspaper interview to a Newark newspaper. The Newark police then arrested him on the street.

If Eleanor and George had seen the film in Chicago, Eleanor would have learned that even in the worst situations, escape from prison was possible. In December 1932, with the real-life Burns in police custody, movie-goers wondered if he could avoid extradition to Georgia where he still was a wanted man. In the film, Burns was told by another inmate, "You gotta watch; you gotta wait." Like Bonnie and Clyde, Burns had (for some) become a folk hero too.

Eleanor and George may well have been influenced by their contemporaries. By the spring of 1933, Bonnie and Clyde were holed up with Clyde's brother and wife in a hideout in Joplin, in southwestern Missouri. Residents, especially in the Midwest, wondered where they would strike next. The gang were emulated and feared, and they got plenty of newspaper coverage. Readers even learned that Bonnie had dyed her hair red when she was "on the lam." She was identified as Clyde's moll, a gangster's girlfriend, perhaps inspiring Eleanor to become a gangster's moll as well.

CHICAGO ROBBERIES

As the newspapers continued to follow the exploits of Bonnie and Clyde, as well as fugitive Robert Elliott Burns, reports of robberies by an unidentified man and a woman began to trickle into different precincts of Chicago. Although neither person in the following newspaper items was identified, these robberies may have marked the beginning of Eleanor and George's partnership. On January 16, 1933, the *Chicago Tribune* published the following very short news brief titled "Girl Helps in Robbery of Devon Avenue Store":

> *A girl assisted a two-gun bandit in a robbery at the fruit store at 1614 Devon Avenue last night. She pushed Peter Poulous, the owner, into the basement while her companion threatened him with two guns, then rifled the case drawer of thirty-five dollars [more than $800 today].*

Then, nearly a month later, the same newspaper reported, "Gunwoman's Visit Takes Ole Out of Circulation":

> *A blonde gunwoman and a male companion invaded the room of Ole Knutson, 1050 Buena Avenue, yesterday and robbed him of his Sunday suit, overcoat, seven dollars [more than $160 today], and a camera. The woman also picked up Knutson's only other pair of pants. He grabbed one leg and tugged. She also tugged. The pants ripped and the two bandits left, laughing at their victim's plight.*

LEO JOINS THE PAIR

In both cases, news reports featured the girl/gunwoman. Also common to both cases was the fact that the victims were middle-aged immigrants. Peter Poulous, proprietor of the North Town Food Shop, had come from Greece in 1914. He was single and boarded in the home of a German immigrant jewelry salesman. Ole Knutson, a painter who also was a single boarder, had moved to the United States from Sweden in 1900.

These robberies, in the early months of 1933, occurred within three miles of George's sister's apartment in North Chicago. If Eleanor was the "girl/gunwoman" and George was her "companion," George previously may have been involved in robberies on his own and then tested Eleanor by taking her on a spree in his former neighborhood. If so, they soon expanded their partnership to include a third member—former boxer, Leo Minneci (aka "Joe Miller"). Eleanor had known him first, but George didn't meet Leo until April 1933 when the two men briefly worked together on a Civilian Conservation Corps (CCC) "relief job." The Works Progress Administration (WPA), another federal public works program during the Great Depression, was initiated that same year.

By June 1933, Chicago newspaper readers learned of a new wave of shopkeeper robberies carried out by an unidentified woman and *two* unidentified men. Throughout the summer, the robbers became more brazen, as they inched closer to the Austin neighborhood. Formerly a country village and then a suburban settlement, the Austin community had been annexed into the city of Chicago in 1899. By 1920, the area was well served by streetcars and the Lake Street "L," an elevated railway. In 1930, many of Austin's 130,000 residents were independent shopkeepers who lived in apartments upstairs from their places of business.

Although police reports circulated throughout the city, the robberies during the summer of 1933 caught the attention of Chicago Police Captain Willard L. Malone. In these "daylight robberies," as they were called, the woman and the two men shopped like any other patrons if there were customers in a store, but they held up the shopkeeper if they determined that he or she was alone. The *Chicago Tribune*'s crime statistics at the time showed that the city averaged 1,344 robberies per month, but only one out of every twenty-five robbers were convicted. The police and the public had the same question: How could the robbers be stopped when the odds were so much in their favor?

CAPTAIN MALONE

Chicago Police Captain Willard L. Malone usually could be found at his large oak desk on the second floor of the District 28 Police Station, at 5317 West Chicago Avenue. In theory, being above the ground floor allowed the captain to concentrate on administrative tasks rather than deal with the day-to-day comings and goings in the reception area. He also managed to maintain some distance from his precinct's four patrol cars that all too often pulled into and went out from their bays within the small, but still functional, brick building.

The sixty-four-year-old portly career officer was tough on crime. As he flipped his calendar to August 1933, he reviewed his robbery reports again, looking for any clues of the criminals' identifications. What he didn't know was that the police department was only an eight-minute drive to the apartment where the unidentified woman lived with her partner. And that apartment was only six blocks from 4834 West Monroe Street where the captain lived with his wife and thirty-nine-year-old son, also a police officer. An avid newspaper reader, the captain knew that Bonnie and Clyde hadn't been caught yet either, but at least the police knew who they were.

THE VICTIMS

When Captain Malone finished leafing through his reports, he learned that most of the victims continued to be middle-aged, hard-working immigrants from European and Eastern European countries. Abandoning their native countries, they had come to America to realize the American dream. The more than three dozen robbery reports included the names of the victims, along with brief descriptions of their stolen items. Some of these police reports, as accessed through case files CR-70150 through CR-70155 of the Criminal Court of Cook County, are reflected here. (Newspaper accounts sometimes differed, as reporters often inflated the values of the stolen items.)

- Tuesday June 13, 1933, at 11:30 a.m.—Mrs. Anna Soll (various spellings, but originally Solomonovitz), a forty-eight-year-old Polish immigrant with a third-grade education, owned a dry goods store at 3714 West Chicago Avenue. Two men and a woman tied her up, put a dress over her head, and robbed her of $25 (more than $570 today).
- Wednesday June 28, 1933, at 2:15 p.m.—Two men and a woman entered Mayfield Dry Goods Store at 5345 West North Avenue and stole an unspecified amount of money and/or merchandise from employee F. E. Georgeson.

Then, on both July 1 and July 3, the unidentified woman and the two unidentified men held up two businesses in one day. Obviously, they needed a car to get from one place to the other, as well as a place to store the stolen goods. But no one had seen them come or go, nor were there any reports of suspicious vehicles.

- Saturday July 1, 1933, time not specified—Sarah Gould, a sixty-year-old widow and Norwegian immigrant, managed a boarding house at 675 Sheridan Road. Court documents show that the robbers took $16 in cash (more than $365 today) and three watches that together were valued at $60 (more than $1,370 today). One of the trio brandished a pistol.

- Also on Saturday July 1, 1933, but at 8 p.m.—Adolph Mell, a fifty-five-year-old German immigrant, owned a haberdashery shop at 3622 Fullerton Avenue, north of Garfield Park. The robbers took $82 (more than $1,870 today) in cash, a watch valued at $22 (more than $500 today), and a fountain pen valued at $9 (more than $200 today).

- Monday July 3, 1933, at 11 a.m.—Sophie Hoffman owned a clothing store at 2725 Milwaukee Avenue. According to her report, the unidentified woman took silks and hosiery, as well as children's and women's clothing valued at $200 (more than $4,560 today), while the men stole $14 from the cash register and a ring valued at $25 (together more than $890 today). Sophie also claimed that both men drew guns and the woman "whipped out a blackjack" and struck her over the head.

- An hour later, on Monday July 3, 1933—Fifty-two-year-old Lithuanian immigrant Benjamin Lack, owner of a tailor shop at 4316 West Armitage Avenue, reported that two men and a woman stole $15 (more than $341 today) from his cash register. One of the robbers hit him on his head, slugging him unconscious. The robbers also left with two dresses valued at $15 and three suits of clothing valued at $15 (nearly $700 today).

The rest of the robberies in July and into August were scattered throughout various parts of the city, but none were more than a few miles from Captain Malone's District 28.

- Tuesday July 4, 1933, 12:30 p.m.—Joseph F. Hrejsa, a forty-five-year-old pharmacist of Czechoslovakian heritage and owner of a drug store at 2859 South Crawford Avenue (now South Pulaski Road) reported that two men and a woman took $131 in cash, a watch valued at $20, and three jars of (presumably face) cream valued at $1.50 (all together more than $3,550 today).

- Friday July 21, noon—Grace Rutledge, a fifty-five-year-old Irish immigrant and owner of the Better Value Shops, Inc. selling clothing, hosiery, and lingerie at 609 West Diversey Parkway, stated that two men and a woman stole $21 in cash, fifteen pairs of hose at forty cents per pair, and two dresses worth $20 each (all together more than $1,530 today).

- Also in July (date and time not known)—Ruth Menci (Mencel), owner of a department store at 5241 Fullerton Avenue, stated that she, too, was robbed by two men and a woman. Her losses were not specified.

- Wednesday August 2 at 2:45 p.m.—Joe Nosarzewski, a forty-seven-year-old Polish immigrant in the Brighton Park neighborhood, was robbed of an unspecified amount at his men's clothing store at 4249 South Archer Avenue.

One can easily imagine Captain Malone reflecting on the shop-keepers like Joe who were hit the hardest. They often worked alone and invested nearly all their time, energy, and money in their small family-run businesses. A year earlier, the *Chicago Tribune* published a photograph of several of the store owners holding guns, noting that the police gave them pointers on how to protect themselves.

War on Crime

At this time, a *Chicago Tribune* article had just announced the Criminal Court of Cook County's new "war on crime." The well-publicized crackdown, proposed by the county court's chief justice, John Prystalski, had been prompted by a then-recent murder of a Chicago police officer in the judge's courtroom. A defendant, with a handgun thought to have been smuggled into court by his mother, was seated in a detention room and shot the officer in a futile attempt to escape. The officer had been the ninth police officer to die in the line of duty between January 1 and the date of the article, July 28, 1933.

Within this same time period, the chief justice and his staff scheduled seventy-three murder cases and many more robberies to be "disposed of at once." Then, on Friday August 4, 1933, when the police and the public may not have thought that crime in their neighborhood could get any worse, the telephone rang.

FRIDAY AUGUST 4, 1933

Shortly after 2 p.m., Captain Malone took a call from James Swoik (shortened from Slawikowski), manager of the Father and Son Shoe Store at 4050 West North Avenue. The manager had been alone in his store when two men and a woman robbed him of $80 in cash. The robbers also took a watch valued at $15 and two fountain pens valued at $1 each (all together more than $2,210 today). Oddly, there was no mention of five pairs of men's shoes that a newspaper reporter had noted also were missing. One of the robbers was armed with a pistol.

The shoe store owner begged and pleaded with the captain to arrest the perpetrators. Again, Captain Malone notified his men to be on the lookout. Beginning in 1930, each squad car in the Chicago Police Department's 110-car fleet had been equipped with a radio receiver tuned to radio station WGN. A dispatcher at the police station then was able to interrupt public broadcasts with emergency messages, such as a request for a particular patrol officer to call the Chief Detective's Office at once. To make the call, however, the officer had to get out of his car, find an emergency call box on the street, and then dial the operator to connect him with the chief or a member of his staff. Even with these then-modern advances in communication, reports of the daylight robberies hadn't traveled quickly enough to enable officers to apprehend the robbers.

Captain Malone did, however, get a little more of the robbers' descriptions from the victims. All agreed that the alleged criminals appeared to be in their late twenties or early thirties. One of the men had dark hair, and the other man was slightly taller and a little paunchy. The woman was petite, slender, and blonde. Each of the victims emphasized that the robbers didn't hide their faces or try to conceal or disguise their looks with stocking caps or bandanas. Instead, like Bonnie and Clyde, they appeared emboldened by their latest successes, almost taunting the shopkeepers with their recklessness. None of their victims had fought back.

Fresh on newspaper readers' minds was an editorial cartoon on the front page of the July 28, 1933, *Chicago Tribune* that showed eight disheveled men standing in a row. Above them the artist had drawn an assortment of eight animals—a vulture, rat, hyena, snake, wolf, leopard, alligator, and a skunk. Above, in bold text, a caption read, "We should learn to judge our criminals by their inward resemblance to animals rather than by their outward resemblance to human beings." There was no drawing of a woman, nor was there a picture of a tiger, but those images would come very soon.

CHAPTER 4

Murder and Identification

FORTY MINUTES AFTER CAPTAIN MALONE GOT OFF THE PHONE WITH the shoe store owner, a frantic and breathless Austin neighborhood resident called the police station to report a shooting. He and several others, he said, were outside of 5948 West Division Street, near North Austin Boulevard, and saw a fight, then heard gunshots and witnessed two men and a woman speed away in a blue sedan. Meanwhile, seventy-one-year-old Gustav Hoeh lay bleeding and injured on the sidewalk.

The captain clenched his fist and slammed it on his desk. Had the same unidentified robbers struck again and gotten away twice on the very same day? At least the owner of the shoe store was unhurt, but what was the fate of Hoeh, the proprietor of a men's clothing store?

GUSTAV HOEH

The dispatcher at the Austin Police Station radioed his patrol officers in their automobiles. While most of the officers on the day shift pursued the speeding sedan, another officer went directly to the scene of the crime, intending to transport the injured man to a hospital. But before the officer could get there, a newsboy hailed a passing Ford truck. The driver of the truck pulled over, opened his passenger door, laid out a blanket, and, with the assistance of two other men, placed the victim on the seat.

The newsboy jumped in the back of the truck, then the driver rushed toward Chicago's West Suburban Hospital. Meanwhile, Officer Edwin D. Grant, a member of the West Park Police Department, had been directing traffic at North Austin Boulevard and West Chicago Avenue.

Although he was four blocks away, he heard shouting and went to help. He jumped in the truck as well. Later, the Park Police officer testified that Hoeh, the injured man, was unconscious, bleeding freely, and had been unable to talk and/or give any information. When he reached the hospital, the Cook County deputy coroner pronounced him dead. Of all the robberies attributed to the unidentified men and the woman, Hoeh had been the only victim to fight back. He was the only shopkeeper who died while defending his store.

For the previous eight-and-one-half years, Hoeh had worked in the shop alone, and he and his wife Carrie lived in an apartment behind the shop. At the time of the shooting, Carrie had gone out, but when she returned home, officers F. H. Smith and H. C. Olson, from the Chicago Police Department's Bureau of Investigation, were taking photos, interviewing witnesses, and documenting the crime scene both within the store and out on the sidewalk. The officers dusted the store's interior for fingerprints, but they were unable to obtain any they could use for purposes of identification. Hoeh's eyeglasses had fallen into an open shirt box on the counter, and the glass in the showcase was broken, perhaps, as was speculated, with the butt of a gun. Then there was discussion as to who owned the gun. Carrie would later testify that her husband never had one in his possession.

The initial police report that arrived on Captain Malone's desk attempted to describe the chaos, but it had been written in a hurry and contained major errors, including a statement that the victim had been stabbed. "Mr. Gustave Hack [sic]," an officer had written, "was shot and stabbed and killed while resisting a robbery at a dry goods store at 5848 West Division St." The report also claimed that $300 (worth more than $6,800 today) had been stolen, but, later, no money or merchandise was found to be missing.

Hoeh had been a well-liked and well-respected member of his community. Newspaper accounts described him as "a stocky man and active past the average for his age." He had been in business for twenty-five years and was considered a "neighborhood pioneer." In addition to his wife, he left two grown sons and their families. The owner of a restaurant across the street told a *Chicago Tribune* reporter, "Every morning, in good weather, after he had opened up his shop, Mr. Hoeh used to stand outside the door. I used to watch him. It seemed that his arm was never still, waving to friends as they passed—men and women, and children on their way to school."

ELEANOR A "TIGRESS"

Even before the courtroom drama unfolded and the perpetrators were identified, the two men and, especially, the woman were smeared by the press. Attorneys later would argue that although sensationalized newspaper reports may influence a jury, journalistic scruples were not of concern to reporters competing for a big scoop. The following day's *Chicago Tribune* ran a story titled "Merchant of 70 is Slain by Girl Robber's Gang." Another reporter wrote, "A blonde young woman *with the savagery of a tigress* [author's emphasis], accompanied by two gunmen, shot, stabbed, and slugged Gustav Hoeh, 70 [*sic*] years old yesterday, when he resisted their attempt to rob his haberdashery."

The article, along with dozens more that were reprinted and syndicated all over the country, contained escalating misinformation, with some duplicating the existing errors and others emphasizing that Eleanor really was the "gang's" leader. Three weeks later, some of these contradictions would be brought out in the defendants' trial in the Cook County Criminal Court. While their not-guilty pleas would fall on deaf ears, the "tigress" nomenclature stuck like glue to the still unnamed and unapprehended woman.

WITNESSES TO THE SHOOTING

In the confusion of the shooting, some witnesses said they had heard two shots, while others said three or four. The witnesses also had varying descriptions of the three perpetrators. All, however, agreed that they were white and had escaped in a dark blue Chevrolet sedan with a light blue stripe. Of the two men and the one woman, the Chicago police summarized the statements they were given and came up with the following descriptions:

No. 1. "35 [age in years], 5–7 [height in feet and inches], 180 [weight in pounds], stocky build, brown hair, white shirt, tan pants, carried B. S. revolver."

No. 2. "Woman, 27 [age in years], 5–4 [height in feet and inches], 110 [weight in pounds], slender build, brown hair, blue dress, white trim at neck."

No. 3. "5–4 [height in feet and inches], dark coat, no other description."

Additional details on the woman mentioned her "light complexion" and white hat. The man with the revolver had "bushy" hair, no hat, and had a "full face." The other man wore a gray suit and cap.

The first witness to talk with police was Mae Swanson, whose husband owned a tailor shop across West Division Street. An officer at the 28th District station wrote up her statement as follows:

Mrs. [Mae] Swanson was standing in front of her husband's shop when she heard some screaming and then three or four shots. She then saw a man running from 5948 West Division Street, followed by the deceased who grabbed him, and while he had ahold of him, she saw another man and woman run out of the store behind the deceased. The woman pulled the deceased away from the first man that came out, and they all then jumped into a Chevrolet sedan (about a 1928 model, dark blue, with a light blue stripe around the center of same), drive west on Division Street to Austin Boulevard and turn north on Austin and disappear. She stated that she would be able to identify the first man that came out of the store, as she took particular pains to get a good look at him when he turned and pulled the pistol from his pocket and fired at the deceased. She is not sure that she would be able to identify the other man and the woman.

The police report did not include an erroneous comment that, the next day, a *Chicago Tribune* reporter would attribute to Mae Swanson. When writing of Gustav Hoeh, the reporter misquoted Mae Swanson as saying, "The *woman* struck him down." Another witness statement read:

> *Estelle Rogers and John Brabec were riding in their auto and stopped at Division Street, on Austin Boulevard, for the stop light when they noticed a crowd of people hollering just east of Austin Boulevard. They saw a car pull away from the scene and thinking it might be a hit-and-run car, they took after same, following it for a considerable distance, when they pulled up alongside the car and the driver of the same opened the door and asked them what was all the trouble about. They, becoming scared, left his car and drove back to the scene of the trouble where they then found out that it had been a robbery and a shooting. They stated that this car contained two men and a woman, and that they could positively identify the driver of same.*

1928 CHEVROLET

Figure 4.1. The getaway car driven by Leo Minneci was similar to this image of a 1928 Chevrolet sedan. Author's collection.

They also gave police the license plate number of the getaway car—Illinois 790748.

LEO AND HIS BROTHER

A police detective tracked the license plate number to Emil Minneci, a twenty-one-year-old student at the University of Illinois. When officers went to Emil's apartment, the car was not there. A police "detail" was placed at the address, with instructions to bring in the car and anyone found in it. Meanwhile, a "persons-wanted message" was sent out for the car and its occupants, with instructions to arrest and hold anyone who tried to report the car as stolen.

When Emil, the car's owner, arrived home, police took him to the Chicago Police Department's Detective Bureau, at 1121 South State Street, for questioning. Emil, though, had an alibi. The previous day, when Hoeh was shot, he had worked all day as a clerk at an A & P grocery store. He did tell police that his twenty-seven-year-old brother, Leo Minneci, had come to the store and asked to borrow his car. Emil said that he refused, but Emil did, however, give Leo's address to the police. Leo later contradicted Emil's statement by saying that his brother had given him the car after he (Leo) gave Emil $50 for a new tire. Either way, the car was gone.

Leo was gone too. On Friday August 4, 1933, the day of Hoeh's murder, detectives Edward Dooley and Donald Coakley went to Leo's home at 3346 West Monroe Street and waited with the man's wife Tina and the couple's three children. The family had little to eat and were hungry, so the officers sent out for food. Gradually, the police officers gained Tina's trust, and she gave them the names of Leo's partners—Eleanor Jarman and George Dale, aka "George Kennedy." Tina, described in another newspaper report as "a thin, tiny, little woman," admitted that shortly after the shooting, she had gone to Eleanor and George's apartment at 4300 West Madison Street looking for her husband. She found him there, along with "Mrs. Jarman and the Jarman children."

"Leo's hand was bandaged, and he told me he had been in some trouble," Tina told the officers. "Then he gave me the keys to the car, and he told me to give the keys to Emil and tell him to report the car stolen.

Mrs. Jarman was packing up, and she left in a taxi with her children." Had Eleanor, previously, left the children home alone? LeRoy was eleven years old at the time, and LaVerne was nine. One has to wonder, too, if the police attempted to contact the driver of the taxi. Later, however, however, the police did search the West Madison Street apartment and confirmed that its inhabitants had "recently fled."

Detectives Dooley and Coakley stayed at Leo's apartment all night following Hoeh's murder. The next morning, on Saturday, August 5, at 10:30 a.m., Leo telephoned his wife and told her that he had spent the previous night on the ground in a "prairie." According to later court testimony, Detective Dooley took the phone and said to Leo, "Listen, we know where you are, and we'll catch up with you. When we do, we're going to shoot first and ask questions later. You'd better surrender and save your life."

Leo's telephone conversation with the officers left him shaken, and the gunshot wound in his hand was giving him a lot of pain. Knowing the police were looking for him, he agreed to give himself up. The officers apprehended him that evening, at 10 p.m., in front of the Bell Telephone building at the intersection of West Madison Street and North Homan Avenue, on the east side of Garfield Park. Leo then asked to see his wife and children, so the officers drove him to his home and allowed him ten minutes with his family. Then they took him to the Detective Bureau. There, in an interrogation room, he met with Chief of Detectives William V. Blaul who began formal questioning at 10:50 p.m.

In admitting that he had been present at Hoeh's murder, Leo also told the chief that he had been shot when he tried to keep "Kennedy" from shooting the storekeeper. He claimed that he had no actual part in the crime, and that "Kennedy" had pulled the trigger. The more Leo talked, though, the more he strayed from the truth. He told the chief of detectives that before arriving at Hoeh's shop, he, Eleanor, and George were just out for a drive and on their way to a baseball game. However, the trio's minutes-before robbery at the Father and Son Shoe Store clearly disproved his story. Adding to his already shaky account, there had been no Cubs game at Wrigley Field that day.

Leo's August 5, 1933, statement to police ("People's Exhibit 14") was published by the Supreme Court of the State of Illinois, December Term A.D. 1933, in *The People of the State of Illinois vs. George Dale, otherwise known as George Kennedy; Eleanor Jarman, and Leo Minneci*. Leo was asked to substitute "the man" for George Dale and "the woman" for Eleanor Jarman. The statement read, in part:

> *When I got to Division Street, the man said turn right, and we then went down to Division Street until we got to Austin Boulevard and when he seen the Hoeh store he said, "Wait a minute until I go in and get a shirt." So, we all went in to pick out a shirt.*
>
> *The old man, Gustav Hoeh said, "Well, what can I do for you?" The man said that he wanted to see some shirts. Gustav Hoeh showed him some cheap shirts first and the man said he wanted to see some more expensive shirts. As the fellow had five or six boxes out on the counter, the man put a gun up to the old man's side and said, "This is a stickup." The old man started to fight with the man, and I was trying to pull the man away, and he hit me with the butt of the gun on my right hand. He either shot me or accidentally shot me on my left hand.*
>
> *When I seen my left hand bleeding, I ran out to the car which was parked in front of the store facing west. I then heard three or four shots as I was in the driver's seat, and then the man and the woman got in the car as I was starting it. I had a hard time to start it, and the man said, "Let's go, drive north," so I turned north into Austin Boulevard, turned to my left at the first street, and as there was another car following us. I stopped the car and asked the people what they wanted. They said, "All right, go ahead, we have the license number."*
>
> *I then went to my left at the next turn and back to Austin Boulevard and turned south again. At this point we were at Quincy and Adams, west of the viaduct. The man said, "Stop and leave the car." I agreed, as I was full of blood from my left hand which was bleeding very badly. We left the car at this point and walked to the man's house. The man said I am going home, and the woman said come on up to my place and fix your hand, which I did.*

After she fixed it with some rags which she had, I decided not to go home, as I was weak from the loss of blood, so I took a streetcar and went west on Madison Street and got off at Cicero Avenue and went north on Cicero to Grand Avenue, got a Grand Avenue streetcar and went all the way to the end of the line. In the meantime, I was weak from the loss of the blood, so I stopped in a drug store located at about 7200 West Grand Avenue and got some bandages and iodine and salve, and I then walked west on Grand Avenue to a prairie near Westwood and then treated and fixed my hand.

After doing this I stayed there and slept on the grass, thinking of what a dirty trick was pulled on me and thinking about my wife and children. I then decided to give myself up and still walked around thinking it over. I called my wife and talked to her and then to Officer Dooley of the Detective Division. Officer Dooley advised me to give myself up, so I told Officer Dooley that I would meet him in front of the Bell Telephone Company on Homan Avenue, south of Madison Street. I met Officer Dooley and his partner Officer Coakley at this point and was escorted to the Detective Division.

Coroner's Inquest

Also on August 5, the day after the murder and while the detectives were still waiting in Leo's apartment with his family, the Cook County's deputy coroner held an inquest. At 9:30 a.m., at Schilke's Morgue, he met with six men "duly sworn to inquire on the part of the People of the State of Illinois into all circumstances attending the death of said dead body." The deputy coroner was required to address the "how and in what manner, and by whom or what, and when and where the said dead body came to its death."

After examining Hoeh's body and the evidence, the jurors concluded "that the dead body now or then lying at 5839 West North Avenue in said City of Chicago, County of Cook, State of Illinois, came to its death on the 4th day of August A.D. 1933 as the result of gunshot wounds of [the] chest, [as well as] shock and hemorrhage." Later, at Eleanor, George, and Leo's trial, a consulting physician would testify that Hoeh also had a one-half-inch laceration on the back of his head.

35

The "Coroner's Verdict Card," though, simply read, "Shot and killed by holdup men—murder." A longer version continued as follows:

> *Said wounds received while the deceased was resisting an attempt[ed] holdup in his haberdashery store located at 5948 West Division Street, and in the struggle with these holdup men and one woman was slugged and shot by them who then escaped in an automobile on the 4th day of August A.D. 1933, about 2:40 p.m. From the testimony presented, we the jury believe this occurrence to be murder, so we recommend the police continue their search for said unknown persons and when apprehended they be held to the grand jury on a charge of murder until resolved by due process of the law.*

CLOSING IN

On August 7, three days after Hoeh's murder and two days after Emil Mennici's arrest, officers Smith and Olson, from the Chicago Police Department's Bureau of Identification, found the Chevrolet sedan at 4541 West Monroe Street. It was parked only three blocks from the home of Captain Malone. The officers again dusted for fingerprints and found some "suitable for identification purposes" on the glass window of the automobile's right door. They also took three photographs of the sedan and sent them to the Bureau's chief of detectives.

But what of Mrs. Jarman, her children, and the man known as "Kennedy"? Every day, newspaper readers were kept up to date on the intense manhunt for the alleged murderers. What the public didn't know, however, was that the police continued to question Leo not only about Eleanor Jarman and George Dale (aka "Kennedy") but also about their acquaintances. Leo's repeated questioning led to the name of Eleanor's *former* live-in boyfriend—a man who later would be acknowledged as Eleanor's "very close friend." Was he involved and, if so, how?

With the tip-off from Leo, two police detectives went to the former boyfriend's apartment at 32 South Kedzie Avenue. No one was home, but a janitor let them in. Inside, they found a dog, along with three pairs of new shoes bearing the same brand as the ones that were stolen (on the day of Hoeh's murder) from the Father and Son Shoe Store. One of the detectives, without divulging the former boyfriend's name, was quoted about the man in "Tiger Woman! Murder by Gun Girl and Two Companions"—a *Chicago Tribune* article that recapped the case a few years later (on December 15, 1935). The following is an excerpt:

> *"My partner and I waited in the apartment with the dog and the three pairs of shoes for two days and two nights," one of the detectives told a newspaper reporter. "Then we were rewarded. The man who occupied the apartment returned. In the pocket of the suit he wore, we found a ticket he had purchased when he crossed a toll bridge over the Mississippi River. His car was muddy and dirty."*

The detectives told the man that if he withheld any information from them that they later learned elsewhere, he would automatically become an accessory to murder. The police then took him to the police station, where he admitted that he had taken Eleanor's two children to her sister Hattie Stocker's home in Sioux City, Iowa. Eleanor obviously had relied on someone she knew well and whom the boys liked and trusted. Under constant interrogation and likely exhausted from his nearly five-hundred-mile drive back from Sioux City, Eleanor's friend revealed to police that Eleanor and George had moved to a "hideout."

Then the police grilled the man some more—all day and into the evening of August 9. He likely was sleep deprived, and the police may have withheld food and water. Perhaps there were additional and questionable techniques that a turnover of rested and well-fed police officers used in their interrogations. Then, with the "accomplice to murder" charge still hanging over his head, Eleanor's friend gave the officers the information they demanded. One of the detectives wrote in his report:

> *He finally told us that Mrs. [Eleanor] Jarman and [George] Dale [aka "Kennedy"] had rented a room at 6323 Drexel Avenue and were living under the name of Anderson. We took along a dozen policemen and went out there. We went into their second-floor apartment, put our shoulders and feet to the door and broke in.*

CHAPTER 5

Cornered and Questioned

ON TUESDAY AUGUST 8, WHILE ELEANOR'S CHILDREN WERE SETTLING in at their Aunt Hattie's home in Sioux City, Gustav Hoeh's widow, Carrie, slowly climbed the steps of a small chapel at 5839 West North Avenue. Her grown sons, Norman and Earl, one on either side, supported her arms. Carrie was dressed in black, including a black veil that hung down over her face. In the chapel's sanctuary, the immediate family accepted the condolences of extended family and friends. Carrie then made her way to the front pew where she lowered her head in prayer. Perhaps in her hand she, like others from the "old country," clutched a worn but favored handkerchief. Carrie was Norwegian, but her late husband was German. An organist likely played Gustav's favorite German hymn.

After the short funeral service, Carrie, Norman, and Earl rode in a limousine that followed a shiny black hearse up North Austin Avenue. Twenty minutes later, they and others in the funeral procession reached Chicago's Mount Olive Cemetery, founded by the city's Scandinavian descendants. A bell tolled to greet the string of automobiles as the Hoehs and their friends passed through the cemetery's arched entryway.

Meanwhile, funeral attendees reflected on Gustav's kindness and contributions to the neighborhood, but they also talked among themselves about the recent arrest of Leo Minneci. They speculated, as well, on the other man and the woman who remained at large.

WEDNESDAY AUGUST 9

The community didn't have long to wait as the very next day, Wednesday August 9, at 10 p.m., was the day that multiple police officers broke into George and Eleanor's rented room. Commanding the raid was supervising Chicago Police Captain John P. Stege who, four months later, would lead a forty-man squad in search of gangster John D. Dillinger. As reported in the *Chicago Tribune* on August 7, 1933 ("Press Search for Woman in Holdup Murder"), the captain told his officers that "they need not feel squeamish about shooting in case Mrs. [Eleanor] Jarman is cornered." He added, "If she is the woman who has been terrorizing west-side merchants, she's desperate. No matter how we do it, we're going to get her." Captain Stege's "shoot to kill" orders would apply to Dillinger as well.

The show of police force paid off. As two detectives covered Eleanor and George with guns, both surrendered, and Officer Albert Glass arrested them without incident. The police also found and confiscated four revolvers wrapped in a bundle and tied with string, as well as a blackjack (also known as a sap)—a short and weighted weapon used for bludgeoning.

In addition to Captain Stege, five officers from the Austin district and three from district 7, along with Officer Glass and fellow Detective Pat Touhy, were mentioned in police and court reports. Captain Willard Malone was there too, as was his Lieutenant, George Lynch. Articles published in various newspapers gave basically the same information—that the police burst into the room at a prearranged signal.

Of equal interest to reporters, however, was the color of Eleanor's hair. The first post-arrest story in *The Lincoln Star Journal*, in Lincoln, Nebraska, was titled "Gunwoman Dyes Her Hair: Couple Seized for Merchant's Murder." There was no clarification as to whether Eleanor actually held the gun, which she hadn't, but newspaper readers learned that "Mrs. Jarman's hair, described as blonde by witnesses, was a flaming red when she was taken." As had outlaw Bonnie Parker, she dyed it as a disguise.

Still, Eleanor was, and would continue to be, the "blonde tigress."

Police Interrogations

Eleanor and George arrived at the Austin Police Station very late in the evening. Leo was in one of the holding cells, where he'd been for the past four days. Even if he hadn't seen his partners arrive, someone would have told him about their arrests. Eleanor must have wondered what the police said or did to her former boyfriend and employer, as he was the only person who had known where she and George were hiding. After being searched and fingerprinted, and without legal counsel, an officer took Eleanor to Captain Willard Malone's office for her "voluntary statement." No doubt she was nervous and scared as she was confronted by Lieutenant Lynch, Assistant State Attorney William T. Crilley, officers Touhy and Glass, a court stenographer, and one of Hoeh's sons.

Albert Glass, the arresting officer, took Eleanor's statement beginning at 11:58 p.m. She, like Leo, said that the three of them (including George) had been "driving around" before they reached Hoeh's store. She added that, as far as she knew, there was no plan to commit a robbery, but she conveniently neglected to say that the three of them had just robbed the shoe store less than an hour before entering Hoeh's shop. The police and, eventually, the jury would be forced to separate fact from fiction—not just from the press, but from the defendants themselves.

Eleanor began her statement by saying that on the day of the murder, Leo had come to her West Madison Street apartment at 11:30 a.m. or 12 p.m. Fifteen or so minutes later, they were joined by George. Then Leo asked if she wanted to go out for a drive. Later, during her trial, Eleanor would repeat her story to her attorney under direct examination. As published by the Supreme Court of the State of Illinois, December Term A.D. 1933, as *The People of the State of Illinois vs. George Dale, otherwise known as George Kennedy; Eleanor Jarman, and Leo Minneci*, Eleanor's testimony read, in part:

> *I wasn't dressed or anything, and I said, "I don't know." He [Leo] said, "I will go and get my brother's car, and by the time I get back you will be dressed." And George says to me, "Go ahead and get dressed and come with us," and so I got dressed and by the time [Leo] Minneci came back we were going out for a ride and we went out, it seemed*

like it was—I don't know just how far—to the highway, and we
circled away around north and coming back again, came back west
again, but at the time I didn't know it was Division Street, but it
must have been Division Street.

Eleanor then told the police and the others that both Leo and George
started talking about buying shirts. They drove by Hoeh's store, decided
to go in, and parked in front. While Gustav Hoeh was showing shirts to
the men, Eleanor claimed that she had wandered toward the back of the
store where she looked at blue neckties that she wanted to buy for her
boys. She continued:

I walked back by the ties, and it seems I was not there no time when,
all of a sudden, a shot was fired and when I looked around all three
[George, Leo, and Gustav Hoeh] were in a huddle toward the front
door. I got so excited I ran out of the store, and I had to run around
the three of them, huddling in the front doorway to get out. They were
standing there hollering, and I got out in the car. They were fighting or
wrestling. I don't know what they were doing. I really don't remember
what took place after the shot was fired, and in the car—it seems like
I was not there any time at all—when the two men got there and
each came in from opposite sides of the car, one got in the front and
one in the back and we went north. One of the men said, "Hurry the
hell out of here."

THURSDAY AUGUST 10

After Eleanor's initial questioning, Officer Glass locked her into a holding cell and then questioned Leo. A newspaper reporter may have sat
in or read the statements immediately afterward, as the *Chicago Tribune*
gave the details early the next morning. Although not mentioned by the
press, sleep deprivation must have been one of the interrogators' main
investigative techniques, as the officer, who obviously worked the night
shift, began to question Leo at 2:20 a.m., early on Thursday, August 10.
Then, beginning at 3:45 a.m., police obtained a second statement from

Leo, but this time in the presence of George. After that, they got a statement solely from George, beginning at 3:53 a.m.

By questioning Eleanor, George, and Leo separately and then in the presence of each other, the police looked for and noted inconsistencies. In the defendants' rambling and still "voluntary" statements, Eleanor and George attempted to absolve each other from any guilt, while Leo tried to cast blame on them both.

SHOW-UP PLATFORM

Already worn out from their interrogations and lack of sleep, Thursday, August 10, was the first of several even longer days for Eleanor, George, and Leo. The three defendants were put on display on what the police called a "show-up platform." Captain Malone had invited the "daylight robbery" victims and anyone else who felt they had been victimized "to troop through the Austin police station." All day, the three defendants were forced to remain seated in front of a constant stream of viewers.

Sophie Hoffman, who had been robbed in July and had reported the theft of women's clothing, was quoted as exclaiming, "The coat she [Eleanor] is wearing now was stolen from my shop!" Readers may wonder why Eleanor would be wearing a "coat" in August, but lightweight coats (called "swagger coats") were the latest in women's fashions and often worn over printed dresses. The police likely had instructed Eleanor, George, and Leo to wear street clothes, and perhaps, in the confusion of the previous evening, the stolen clothing was all that Eleanor had been able to bring along. She also wore a white hat and held her gloves and purse in her lap. George, seated on the platform in the middle, had on a suit and a light-colored cap. Leo wore a straw hat, was jacketless, and rolled up his shirt sleeves.

As quoted by a reporter, another victimized shopkeeper, Robert Shiff, stated, "She [motioning to Eleanor] struck me over the head with a gun. Then they robbed me. I'd know her anywhere." Sophie Hoffman later reminded police that (as noted in her police report) she also had been struck over the head, but with a blackjack. These victims also said that they had heard Eleanor tell her male companions to "slug" them. These comments may or may not have been true, but they would be inadmissible in court as they only pertained the victims' robbery cases and not to the murder of Gustav Hoeh.

Later, after Eleanor was returned to her holding cell, she was interviewed by a *Chicago Tribune* reporter whose upbeat and possibly concocted write-up contradicted a forlorn-looking photo of Eleanor after a day on the show-up platform. Stated the writer:

> *Today she sat, this "tiger woman," all smiles and amiability, dressed in a blue and orange smock, sipping a cup of coffee she poured out of a milk bottle with a steady hand. Her red hair, dyed since the killing of Gustav Hoeh a week ago, flamed brilliantly against the drab walls of her cell. And there, as she sipped nonchalantly, she confessed, very much in earnest, "I'll admit what I did. I'll tell the truth about myself. I must have held up at least ten places. That is all I can remember exactly. There must be more."*

MORE QUESTIONING

On August 10, after having to give a statement in the middle of the previous night, and then sitting on the show-up platform all day, George was asked to give another statement at night, at 11:47 p.m. This time, Eleanor was present. Also present was Assistant State Attorney Crilley, Deputy Chief of Detectives William V. Blaul, officers Touhy and Glass, and a reporter. The reporter wasted no time getting a story in the following day's newspaper telling his avid readers that George claimed he had shot Hoeh in self-defense, but the gun was not his so it must have belonged to the victim. George said the gun discharged when he and Hoeh were struggling for its possession. This statement (People's Exhibit 15) was referenced, as follows, also by the Supreme Court of the State of Illinois, in its December Term, 1933. But the reference was stated in a separate document (from the before referenced Illinois Supreme Court document) specifically prepared as a *Brief and Argument for Plaintiff in Error:*

> *In this statement, Dale said he had been treated well by the police officers; had been given no promise of reward or immunity, and that he knew that anything he said might be used against him. He says*

Figure 5.1. This photo was taken the day Eleanor wore the blue and orange dress, and it clearly shows her dark hair, dyed red at the time. Chicago Tribune Historical Photos/TCA.

Figure 5.2. During a lighter moment, Eleanor gave a newspaper photographer a rare smile. Chicago Tribune Historical Photos/TCA.

that he went to Eleanor Jarman's house at 4300 West Madison Street on Friday morning about ten o'clock and that Joe (meaning, no doubt, Minneci) was there already. They said they would go out for a ride. They went to a filling station and then went north to Division Street and stopped at a store to buy a shirt. They did not have the number he wanted, and Joe asked for a shirt, too.

They were looking at sweaters and an argument started, and they got to shuffling around and Hoeh had a gun. The gun was accidentally discharged, and it was accidentally discharged a second time when they got to the front door and, to use the language of the witness, "So that the three of us, we didn't have anything, she was not in it at all; she cleaned away from us; she did not even know what was going on at that time."

Leo Minneci, in the presence of defendant said, "Eleanor must have given the gun to George because George said, 'Stick them up' and pulled the gun." When he [Minneci] pulled Dale's arm away, Dale shot him through the hand and twisted and hit Hoeh on the head. He did not see Hoeh have any gun. Dale did say that there was a gun there but does not say who had it and that they were all scuffling for it. Mrs. Jarman said to him, "Don't be a fool. He had the gun, or you had the gun." She does not know who fired the shot and did not know who had the gun.

Eleanor stuck with her story that she was in the back of the store when she heard a shot and said, "That's all I know about it." Every statement, including this one, seemed to have its own contradictions that included George giving 4300 Madison Street as his address, but also stating that he went to "Eleanor's house" at 4300 Madison. When Officer Glass brought in Leo to confront the pair, Leo said, as noted earlier, that George drew a gun and announced a robbery. George, however, wasn't wearing a jacket, and Leo claimed that George had no place to conceal a gun, so Leo then concluded that Eleanor must have had the gun in her purse and then given it to George. The only facts that were made clear were that Leo really had been shot in the hand, and they all fled together in Leo's brother's Chevrolet sedan.

FRIDAY AUGUST 11
Eleanor's photo from the first day on the show-up platform appeared in local and national newspapers on Friday, August 11, one week after the shooting. She wore the blue and orange dress, her hair was neatly coiffed, her eyebrows thinly plucked, and she had on dark lipstick. Headlines varied, but all were along the lines of "the blonde tigress" being identified by many victims.

That evening, the three defendants were on display yet again, but this time at the Detective Bureau. As the newspapers stated, they were "paraded with thugs and thieves." The experience must have been sobering, as Eleanor downplayed her involvement when interviewed by another newspaper reporter the following day. She insisted she was "no tiger woman," but merely an innocent bystander when Hoeh was murdered. By that time, however, twenty-three recent victims of northwest-side robberies had positively identified her and her two male companions as "bandits who specialized in daylight holdups."

During the time that victims were invited to view the defendants, newspaper readers were (erroneously) reminded again that Eleanor had *stabbed* Gustav Hoeh. Reporters did, however, continue to push the narrative that Eleanor had kicked the victim about the head and on his face. George's story, that he had wrestled a revolver from Hoeh's hands and shot in self-defense, began to collapse after Leo was asked to view the four revolvers and the blackjack that were found in Eleanor and George's hideout. Leo pointed out a .38 caliber revolver and said it was the murder weapon. Police then sent the gun to the Northwestern University Crime Detection Laboratory for ballistics tests.

Further inflating the "tigress" depiction, several of the witnesses described Eleanor as "the most ferocious of the trio." The police had initially referred to her as "a cake of ice" and said she "denies it all." The press agreed, stating that she had "a hard-boiled attitude, shrugging her shoulders as the identifications came in and stating a few more won't make any difference." But according to one newspaper reporter, Eleanor moaned, "Oh, what will become of my poor little boys? Who will take care of them now?" The cake of ice, if it ever existed, was beginning to crack.

MORE SHOW-UPS

On Saturday, August 12, after Eleanor, George, and Leo spent a third day on the show-up platform, the number of residents who claimed to have been victimized by the defendants had risen to thirty-seven. Because prior crimes were not admissible in court, Eleanor, George, and Leo may have wondered why they constantly were on display. Later they learned that the prosecutor needed to prove that the three of them had been seen together in other shops. Perhaps another hoped-for outcome, as any viewer of the *Perry Mason* television series can attest, would be a courtroom confession—if not to the murder of Gustav Hoeh, then to one or more of the robberies.

Sunday, August 13, was the last day that Eleanor and the others had to sit on the platform and be viewed as spectators passed by and stared.

But on that day, Eleanor was confronted by Anna Soll, her thirty-eighth victim. Anna was the dry goods store owner who claimed that Eleanor had tied her up, then covered her head with a dress. After Anna pointed her out at the police station, a *Chicago Tribune* reporter noted, "Her [Eleanor's] spirit appeared broken. A police matron had to support her, and she was half-lifted to the show-up platform. Her eyes were red from crying, and she broke into sobs when she was identified."

Figure 5.3. Captain Willard L. Malone questioned Eleanor about the guns his officers had confiscated in the Drexel Avenue "hideout." Chicago Tribune Historical Photos/TCA.

PART II

TRIAL

CHAPTER 6

Preliminary Proceedings

ON SUNDAY, AUGUST 13, THE LAST DAY THAT ELEANOR, GEORGE, AND Leo had to sit on the "show-up" platform, news of Eleanor's arrest reached her hometown of Sioux City, Iowa. Readers of the *Sioux City Journal* learned that "Mrs. Eleanor Jarman is held in connection with a murder" and that a relative was caring for her boys. Eleanor knew LeRoy and LaVerne would be safe with her sister Hattie, but how was she answering their questions? Were other children making fun of them at school? The newspaper included a photo of Eleanor's tear-stained face, along with her plea "to think of my poor children."

Eleanor, George, and Leo had never before been locked up or arrested, so spending five days and five nights in holding cells at the Austin Police Station was quite an adjustment from apartment life. But their confinement was nothing like what was to come.

On Monday, August 14, the day after the police had completed their initial investigations, the three defendants were sent, in a paddy wagon, to the Cook County Jail, at 2700 South California Avenue. There they would stay through their joint trial. The stark six-story stone structure had opened in 1929 when Chicago police officials moved 1,341 prisoners in multiple bus loads from the old county jail at Austin Avenue and Dearborn Street. Once inside, George and Leo were taken in one direction, and Eleanor in another. It had to have been a frightening time.

Officials booked the three alleged criminals and took them to their cells. Normally this was the time for inmates to exchange their personal clothing for jail-issued garb, but another arrangement was made that allowed them to wear street clothes in court. As the heavy steel doors clanged behind them, the cold reality of being locked up, alone, hit each of them in the face.

AUGUST 15, INDICTMENT

Preliminary court proceedings began early in the morning of Tuesday, August 15. That same day, newspaper readers in Sioux City saw a smiling photo of Eleanor, along with the headline "Former Sioux City Woman Is Held for Chicago Robberies." Only the text mentioned a murder. Eleanor again joined George and Leo in the back of the paddy wagon. The "new" building of the Criminal Court of Cook County had fourteen courtrooms and had also opened in 1929.

By today's standards, the proceedings were exceedingly swift, as the time from Eleanor's and George's arrests to the end of their trial was only three weeks. At the court building, all three defendants were brought

Figure 6.1. This building of the Cook County Jail opened in 1929. At the time, its population was considered the largest concentration of inmates in the free world. Chicago History Museum DN-0087861, Chicago Sun-Times/Chicago Daily News collection, Chicago History Museum.

before Judge Philip J. Finnegan, one of the court's twenty-one judges. He charged each defendant with one count of murder and six counts of robbery. These criminal court cases are archived in the Office of the Clerk of the Circuit Court of Cook County and were summarized, as follows, by the Chicago Crime Commission:

> *Case No. 70149. Charged with the murder of Gustav Hoeh "in the course of a holdup by shooting the deceased through the heart."*

> *Case No. 70150. Charged with the robbery of Joseph Hrejsa [the druggist on South Crawford Avenue].*

> *Case No. 70151. Charged with the robbery of Benjamin Lack [the owner of a tailor shop].*

> *Case No. 70152. Charged with the robbery of Adolph Mell [the owner of a haberdashery].*

> *Case No. 70153. Charged with the robbery of Sarah Gould [the manager of a boarding house].*

> *Case No. 70154. Charged with the robbery of James Swoik [the owner of the Father and Son Shoe Store that was robbed the same afternoon as the murder of Gustav Hoeh].*

> *Case No. 70155. Charged with the robbery of Grace Rutledge [owner of a store selling women's clothing, hosiery, and lingerie].*

Judge Finnegan immediately assigned Eleanor's, George's, and Leo's seven cases to a grand jury, a group of supposedly impartial citizens who were selected from a list of eligible voters and then summoned by the sheriff of Cook County. After being sworn in, the jurors' duty was to listen to presentations by the prosecutor and his chosen witnesses to determine if there was "probable cause" that a crime or crimes had been committed. The grand jury had several cases on its docket that day, but the murder and robbery charges for Eleanor, George, and Leo were first.

The witnesses for Case No. 70149—the murder of Gustav Hoeh—included one of the victim's sons, Earl Hoeh, as well as four eyewitnesses (Estelle Rogers, Mae Swanson, Vincent Homings, and William Frederick) who saw the shopkeeper while he was being attacked. The witness list also included a large group of police officials. Those from the Austin Police Station's 28th District were Albert Glass (who had arrested Eleanor and George), Patrick Touhy, Ellwood Egan, Edward Considine, and Captain Willard L. Malone. Also testifying were detectives Coakley and Dooley, who had spent a night at Leo's home. Not subpoenaed was Captain John P. Stege, who commanded the raid when the defendants were arrested. He had been brought in, at the time, as the "top gun," even though he did not participate in the investigations.

After the grand jury's deliberation on the murder charge for Gustav Hoeh, the jury foreman handed the judge its written decision—a formal indictment called a "True Bill." The court proceeding indicated that the jury members believed the prosecution had presented enough evidence on the murder to equally indict all three defendants. It should be noted that the phrase "malice aforethought" meant that the accused knew that his or her action would hurt or kill the other person.

The True Bill made the following accusations and read, in part:

- Assaulted—Eleanor, George, and Leo "unlawfully, feloniously, willfully and of their malice aforethought made an assault in and upon the body of one Gustav Hoeh."

- Shot—Eleanor, George, and Leo "discharged and shot off, to, against, towards and upon Gustav Hoeh a certain pistol commonly called a revolver, then and there charged with gunpowder and divers leaden bullets, which pistol Eleanor Jarman and said George Dale and said Leo Minneci each *then and there had and held in their hands* [author's emphasis]."

- Wounded—Eleanor, George, and Leo "struck, penetrated, and wounded said Gustav Hoeh in and upon the chest, trunk, thorax, abdomen, and body of said Gustav Hoeh with two of said leaden bullets."

- Killed and Murdered by Shooting—Eleanor, George, and Leo "did unlawfully with malice aforethought by shooting, kill and murder Gustav Hoeh."

Each of the robbery victims then testified that they had seen Eleanor, George, and Leo in their places of business. In addition, some of the victims claimed that one of the robbers had been armed with a gun, although none of the witnesses ever stated that Eleanor held the gun, as had been indicated. After the indictment for Gustav Hoeh's murder, the grand jury wrote up six more True Bills and set bail at $10,000 for each defendant in each robbery. With no money and the murder charges hanging over their heads, the defendants found it impossible to even consider bail. What the prosecution was intent on getting across was the association among the three defendants—that Eleanor, George, and Leo had, multiple times, been seen together.

After the grand jury completed its deliberations on the six robberies, there still was time in the day for the jury to hear and act on the cases of four additional alleged murderers, all men. In the first case, two men were charged with the murder of a police officer. The other two men attempted to rob a streetcar conductor, then they allegedly murdered him when he resisted. At the end of the day, another judge, Chief Justice Prystalski, ordered the quick arraignment of the "seven indicted as killers." Referencing Eleanor, George, Leo, and the four men, the chief justice stated, "The only way to answer this apparent defiance on the part of the criminal element is speedy trials and punishment."

August 17, Arraignment

The state had appointed Joseph P. Power as George's defense attorney. He served at taxpayers' expense, but Eleanor and Leo each had private attorneys, with A. Jefferson Schultze representing Eleanor and Irving Abrams representing Leo. There was no mention in the newspapers, however, as to how they were paid. Perhaps Attorney Schultze took the case pro bono, but his reason to do so seems unclear. He was a well-experienced criminal attorney who had first practiced in 1915 in the office of famed attorney Clarence Darrow. A later newspaper reference indicated that Attorney Schultze had considered Eleanor guilty as charged.

Eleanor, George, and Leo were arraigned on Thursday, August 17, when Chief Justice Prystalski formally read all the charges against them and then asked the defendants to enter their pleas. On the advice of their attorneys, all pleaded "not guilty" to both the murder and robbery charges. When a *Chicago Tribune* writer reported on their "not guilty" pleas, he told his readers that the defendants did so "despite the fact that the police said they confessed." The police may have interpreted their voluntary statements as "confessions," but they had been made without counsel.

The three defendants' arraignments were followed by the four other indicted and alleged murderers, as well as a fifth man known as the "courtroom slayer." This man, after his previous indictment for murdering a banker, then shot and killed a police officer in a courtroom on July 24. The *Chicago Tribune* reported that he pleaded "not guilty" to this second murder as well. Even his mother entered a "not guilty" plea, then promptly fainted after being charged with aiding her son in his attempted escape by slipping him a revolver in her purse, or "pocketbook."

During the summer of 1933, the crime scene in Chicago had gotten out of control, and the "courtroom slayer's" shooting of the officer precipitated what the police called a "criminal crime campaign." If Eleanor, George, and Leo had been reading the newspapers, they would have known of the police crackdown. Yet they continued their crime spree. What were they thinking? For Eleanor, George, and Leo, their imminent trials couldn't have come at a more difficult time.

Under the headline "Speed Murder Trials of 7 in Crime War," a *Tribune* writer reported that yet another judge, Marcus Kavanagh, "would probably preside over the first of these swift murder trials in the case involving the so-called blonde tigress, Mrs. Eleanor Jarman." Rushing the cases through meant that time was not on the side of any of the defendants. The newspaper reporter explained that, in the past, defense attorneys commonly used standard thirty-day delays to their advantage. What were called "seemingly endless continuances" had come to a screeching halt the previous day when Chief Justice Prystalski, as quoted in the newspaper, "ordered seven persons, one of them a woman [Eleanor], placed on trial for murder within the next two weeks."

Eleanor's attorney, A. Jefferson Schultze, as well as George's and Leo's attorneys, also made their usual thirty-day requests, but they were of no avail. On August 18, 1933, the *Chicago Tribune* printed the courtroom exchanges as follows:

"Did you say five or six days?" asked Judge Kavanagh after the attorneys had made their request.

"No, your honor, we ask for five or six weeks under the Supreme Court decisions," replied Attorney Schultze.

"No, five or six days is more like it," replied the judge firmly. "We will start this case on August 28, a week from Monday. Be ready without further delay."

A QUESTION OF SANITY

After the indictments and arraignments were in place, the court was faced with a question, and that was whether Leo Minneci was fit to stand trial. Chief Justice Prystalski ordered the warden of the Cook County Jail to permit a doctor from the Behavior Clinic of the Criminal Court of Cook County to examine the mental condition of "the above-named defendant [Leo Minneci], now confined in the County Jail." The reason was "a question of sanity." The request had come through a Petition for Severance from one of Leo's brothers, thirty-three-year-old Christ Minneci, himself an attorney, who claimed that Leo's participation in boxing matches had left him mentally incompetent. The severance petition, if granted, would allow Leo to have a trial separate (and, perhaps, more sympathetic) from the trial involving Eleanor and George.

Christ Minneci's letter of August 21, 1933, is included in CR-70149 and reads as follows:

Your petitioner, Christ Minneci, respectfully represents unto this Honorable Court that he is the brother of Leo Minneci, defendant in the above entitled causes, and that he verily believes that the said Leo Minneci is and has been for some years past mentally unsound, and states the fact to be that for some years past the said Leo Minneci has been engaged as a prize fighter under the name of Joe Miller, and as a result of the beatings received about his head during said fights he is what is known to be "punch drunk" as a result of said beatings and has shown a lack of ability to think coherently and to distinguish right from wrong, and at times does not know what he is doing; that said condition is permanent and that as a result of his condition, the Illinois Boxing Commission refused the said Leo Minneci, alias Joe Miller, about five or six months ago, the right to participate in any further boxing matches in the State of Illinois.

The letter continued:

Your petitioner therefore states the fact to be that he believes the said Leo Minneci to be mentally unsound and incompetent and not legally or morally responsible for any acts committed by him, and therefore states that he desires to have the said Leo Minneci examined by certain alienists [psychiatrists who assess the competence of a defendant in a court of law] and physicians and prays that an order be entered directing William D. Meyering, Sheriff of Cook County, to permit Dr. O.A. Kibbler, Dr. A.D. Hershfield, Dr. Anthony Formusa, and Dr. D.A. Palmisano to enter the Cook County Jail for the purpose of examining the said Leo Minneci as to his sanity and to make all tests with reference to his sanity as said alienists and physicians may deem necessary.

Leo's psychiatric report was in the judge's files on August 26, two days before the beginning of the trial. The doctors, including Dr. D. A. Palmisano (who was Leo's brother-in-law), determined, however, that he was sane, so the judge withdrew Leo's brother's severance petition.

DEATH PENALTY

The *Chicago Tribune* announced on Monday, August 28, that, because of the "crime war," all of the state's attorneys for the murder trials during the week would not only seek but "insist on" the death penalty. All would also be jury trials. According to the Cook County Jail's physician, this emphasis on the death penalty threatened many additional still-incarcerated inmates. "In all my experience, I never saw the criminals in such a state of panic," he stated. "The prisoners are actually terror-stricken. They hope the 'war' will be over this week, and then they will be able to bargain again for light sentences in return for pleading guilty or taking bench trials [trials by judges]."

While the trial of the "courtroom slayer" would be held in one courtroom, everything was in place, in another courtroom and on the same day, for Judge Marcus Kavanagh to try the cases of Eleanor, George, and Leo. The prosecutor assigned to their cases was Assistant State Attorney Wilbert F. Crowley. During the prior week, he had prosecuted a man who was sentenced to the electric chair in what was considered the "quickest murder trial in the history of Cook County." Eager to retain his reputation, Attorney Crowley told a reporter, "The thing to do is to put the electric chair to work again to stop all this crime."

CHAPTER 7

Trial, First Two Days

THE HARSH COMMENT OF THE PROSECUTOR—ASSISTANT STATE ATTOR-
ney Wilbert F. Crowley—was picked up by the *Associated Press*, reprinted
in the *Sioux City Journal*, and spread throughout the country. But it was
Eleanor who continued to grab the headlines. On Monday, August 28,
the first day of the joint trial for Eleanor, George, and Leo, the *Chicago
Tribune* announced, "Blonde Tigress and Two Pals Face Court." Even
the titles on many of the court documents read "Eleanor Jarman, et al,"
instead of equally listing all three codefendants. All eyes were on Eleanor
as the court aggressively aimed for a speedy disposition of its cases.

TIMELINE, ALL IN 1933

- August 4—Gustav Hoeh was murdered during an attempted
  robbery.

- August 4—Eleanor and George escaped to their apartment, and
  Leo disappeared.

- August 4—The getaway car's license plate number led to Leo's
  apartment, where his wife gave police the names of Eleanor and
  George.

- August 5—The police raided Eleanor and George's apartment, but
  they had fled.

- August 5—Leo turned himself in to police. His questioning led to
  the name of Eleanor's former boyfriend.

- August 6–7—Eleanor's former boyfriend drove her boys to her sister's home in Sioux City, Iowa. Detectives waited in the man's apartment for his return.

- August 7–8—Eleanor and George hid out in a room on Drexel Avenue.

- August 8—Eleanor's former boyfriend returned from Sioux City.

- August 9—Under lengthy questioning, the former boyfriend gave police the Drexel Avenue address of Eleanor and George's hideout where they were arrested.

- August 10–13—Eleanor, George, and Leo sat on the "show-up platform" at the Austin Police Station.

- August 15—Eleanor, George, and Leo each were indicted for one count of murder and six counts of robbery.

- August 17—Eleanor, George, and Leo were arraigned and pleaded "not guilty."

- August 28—The trial, on day 1 (Monday), included petitions for Eleanor.

- August 29—The trial, on day 2 (Tuesday), included jury selection and instructions.

- August 30—The trial, on day 3 (Wednesday), included prosecution, defense, prosecution's rebuttal, verdict, and motions for new trials.

- August 31—There were no court proceedings on day 4 (Thursday). Eleanor and Leo were interviewed at the Cook County Jail.

- September 1—The trial, on day 5 (Friday), included formal sentencing.

TRIAL PREPARATION

The staff in the prosecutor's office must have worked overtime, as they only had seven business days to get ready—from the defendants' arraignments on August 17 to the beginning of the trial on August 28. First, the prosecution amassed an impressive list of witnesses, then the prosecutor or a staff member called them, one by one, into his office to depose them to find out what they knew of Gustav Hoeh's murder. Some had witnessed the attack (and then attended the "show-up" of the defendants in the police station), while Hoeh's family members could only speak of the man they knew and loved. The testimony of the widow, Carrie Hoeh, was crucial, as she would be asked if her husband had owned a gun.

Also prepared to testify were the deputy coroner, a ballistics expert, and, of course, Captain Willard Malone and his police officers. The captain was proud of his men who had tracked down, arrested, and questioned the three defendants and then compiled the necessary evidence to bring Eleanor, George, and Leo to trial. After the prosecutor heard everyone's accounts, he issued subpoenas to each of the men and women to ensure they would show up in court.

ATTORNEY SCHULTZE'S PETITIONS

The defense team had scrambled to get ready as well. The trial officially began in the Criminal Court of Cook County on Monday, August 28, at 8 a.m. But before the selection of the jury could begin, the morning was filled with additional preliminaries, specifically three petitions initiated by Attorney Schultze for his client, Eleanor. A reporter for the *Chicago Tribune*, obviously biased against the defense, considered the petitions "delay tactics" and called them "excuses for a continuance." The petitions were for:

- A change of courtroom venue regarding judges
- Severance based on a weapon in evidence
- A change of venue to move the trial outside of Cook County

The trial for the codefendants originally was scheduled to go before Judge Marcus Kavanagh. In the Petition for Change of Venue Regarding Judges, Eleanor claimed (and Attorney Schulze wrote) that Judge Kavanagh and another judge were prejudiced against her and that "she fears and believes that she will not receive a fair and impartial trial." In a successful resolution of the petition, Judge Kavanagh was replaced with Judge Philip J. Finnegan.

The Petition for Severance, again written by Attorney Schultze and signed by both him and Eleanor, confirmed that Eleanor had been jointly indicted with George and Leo but that she was requesting a trial of her own. The document stated that Eleanor "verily believes there is certain evidence [specifically the revolver used to kill Gustav Hoeh] which, if introduced in the cause of her trial and were she to go to trial with the above-named defendants, would be prejudicial to her defense and to the cause at hand." In addition, Eleanor and her attorney had concerns that the other defendants might make certain statements that would have a negative influence on the jury. Judge Finnegan denied the severance petition.

The third petition was a Petition for Change of Venue from Cook County. Attorney Schultze again wrote that he did not believe that Eleanor would receive a fair trial, but this time the petition acknowledged blatant sensationalism in the "various newspaper articles that have been published in the newspapers in the City of Chicago, County of Cook and State of Illinois pertaining to your Petitioner's case and also pertaining to the trials of various defendants who have been tried in the Criminal Court." The very real and obvious concern was that recent negative publicity had made it impossible for any judge or jury to be impartial in the upcoming trial.

Attorney Schultze strengthened the Change of Venue petition by attaching two affidavits, each signed by a Chicago resident. One of the signers was Mathew W. Bieszczat, a municipal government worker involved in local politics. The other signer was Richard Slater. The discovery of Richard's name in the court document became a turning point in Eleanor's untold story, as he turned out to be none other than Eleanor's former boyfriend and employer.

Richard's name—in connection with Eleanor—was kept out of the newspapers. Fortunately, however, he signed both his first and last names on the petition, as only his last name, "Slater," would be mentioned in Eleanor's testimony. Although the police had forced Richard to disclose Eleanor and George's hideout under threat of a charge of "accessory to murder," he did attend the trial, and he showed his support. As to his signature on the affidavit, Attorney Schultze probably told him that it would help Eleanor's case, but perhaps Richard also hoped to alleviate some of the guilt he may have felt for contributing to her arrest. Little did Eleanor know, at the time, how much more he would do for her in the future.

Both Richard and the government worker had to swear they were citizens of the United States. Then they were asked for the number of years that they lived in Chicago. For Richard it was thirty-one years, and for Mathew, thirty-two years, their entire lifetimes. Otherwise, their affidavits were identical. Both signed statements stating, in part, "He [the signer] verily believes that the said defendant cannot receive a fair and impartial trial from any jury selected from the County of Cook, State of Illinois, because of the reasons so set forth in the original petition for a Change of Venue." Unfortunately for the defendant, Mathew's and Richard's efforts were to no avail. Judge Finnegan denied that petition too.

At the very same time, and in the same criminal court building, Judge Kavanagh (whom Eleanor and her attorney had dismissed) presided over another murder trial where yet another attorney filed a similar petition for a change of venue out of Cook County. A *Chicago Tribune* reporter followed up on that case and quoted the attorney as stating, "The public was so inflamed by newspaper articles that a fair trial could not be had." The newspaper's reporter even agreed, proudly stating that the *Tribune* itself "is the worst offender." Judge Kavanagh then brushed off the attorney's concerns by commenting, "I think the newspapers have merely awakened the conscience of the people of this county."

JURY SELECTION

August 29 was the day for the "examination of jurors." According to a then-current police manual, a jury was defined as "a body of twelve competent men, disinterested and impartial, not of kin nor personal dependents of either of the parties, having their homes in the jurisdictional limits of the court, drawn and selected by officers *free from all bias* [author's emphasis] in favor of or against either party, duly impaneled and sworn to render a true verdict, according to the law and evidence."

No one, however, explained how they could be "free from all bias" when they continued to be bombarded with newspaper articles on the "blonde tigress."

The defense team of A. Jefferson Schultze representing Eleanor; an assistant public defender, Joseph P. Power (along with a second assistant, Frank J. Ferlic), representing George; and attorney Irving Abrams representing Leo asked for several days to select the jury. Judge Finnegan, however, insisted that his court would remain in session until the jury was sworn in—that same day. As usual, reporters were in the courtroom, and one noted, "The lawyers protested several times that they had pangs of hunger, but the judge kept on until nearly 5 o'clock." The team only chose married men for the jury, and Prosecutor Crowley instructed them "not to be swayed by the fact that a woman is a defendant."

The twelve men selected for the jury were mostly native-born Chicago residents, in age from twenty-five to fifty-nine years old. A few, like the victim Gustav Hoeh, were immigrants. At least four on the jury had less than eighth-grade educations, with one having only completed fourth grade. The three most educated men each had completed four years of high school. The jurors' occupations ranged from clerks and salesmen to laborers, repairmen, and a factory worker. A newspaper reporter in the courtroom noted, "Mrs. [Eleanor] Jarman appeared nervous as the selection of the jury qualified to inflict the death penalty was begun."

In Illinois, women were not allowed to serve on a jury until 1939, but if there had been a woman on this jury, perhaps the male jurors would have better understood the dynamics between Eleanor and George. From all appearances, they were romantically involved, and she likely was economically dependent upon him as well. Eleanor would later state that she followed George's instructions. There was no evidence, at all, of her being the "gang's leader," as several newspaper reports had attempted to portray.

JURY INSTRUCTIONS
After Judge Finnegan swore in the jury, and before they could hear anyone's testimony, he defined several legal terms and presented the men with instructions. Some of these terms included:

- "'Murder' is the unlawful killing of a human being, in the peace of the people, with malice aforethought, either expressed or implied."

- "'Malice' is implied from any deliberate or cruel act against another, however sudden, which shows an abandoned and malignant heart. . . . The words 'malice aforethought' do not necessarily imply the lapse of a considerable time between the malicious intent to take life and the actual execution of that intent."

- "An 'accessory' is he or she who stands by and aids, abets, or assists, or who, not being present, aiding, abetting, or assisting, hath advised, encouraged, aided, or abetted the perpetration of the crime. He or she who thus aids, abets, assists, advises, or encourages, shall be considered as principal and punished accordingly."

- "'Reasonable doubt' is that state of mind which, after a full comparison and consideration of all the evidence, both for the State and the defense, leaves the mind of the jury in that condition that they cannot say that they feel an abiding faith amounting to a moral certainty, from the evidence in this case, that the defendants are guilty of the charge as laid in the indictment."

The charge for all three—Eleanor, George, and Leo—as laid out in the indictment (also known as the "True Bill") was that each of them were principal offenders and "did unlawfully, with malice aforethought by shooting, kill and murder Gustav Hoeh."

The jury instructions went on and on, but some of the instructions, pared down in length and legalese, included the following:

- "You must not allow the gravity of the charge to, in any way, bias your judgement in your deliberations upon a verdict. You must look alone to the evidence and law in this case and from that make your decision. The defendants are entitled to your calm, unbiased, and deliberate judgement upon the truthfulness of the charge against her or him. He or she is presumed by law to be innocent, and this presumption is evidence in his or her behalf

and protects him or her from a conviction until his or her guilt is
established beyond a reasonable doubt."

- "The mere presence of a party near the scene of murder is not sufficient to constitute him or her a principal [offender] unless there
  is something in his or her conduct showing a design to encourage,
  incite, or in some manner aid, abet, or assist in the murder."

- "If the defendant, immediately after the commission of the crime
  with which he or she stands charged, fled and remained away until
  taken into custody, such flight is a proper circumstance to be considered in determining the guilt or innocence of such defendant."

- "Neither the opinion of the prosecuting attorney that the defendants are guilty, nor the opinion of the attorney for the defense
  that the defendants are innocent, should be considered by you as
  evidence of the guilt or innocence of the defendants. It does not
  matter what their opinion may be. Before you can find a defendant guilty you must believe he or she is guilty beyond a reasonable doubt from the evidence as testified to by the witnesses in the
  case and from the testimony in the case."

- "Whoever is guilty of murder shall suffer the punishment of death
  or imprisonment in the penitentiary *for his natural life* [author's
  emphasis], or for a term of not less than fourteen years."

Back in their cells that night, Eleanor, George, and Leo no doubt
were anxious as to what the next day would bring. All were completely
unprepared, however, for the stunning setback that faced not just George,
but all of them. George's public defender, Joseph P. Power, had met several times with George to prepare his defense and was ready to argue
his case the following morning, Wednesday, August 30. But on Tuesday
evening, the defense attorney's father, Pierce B. Power, died at the age of
eighty. His death cast an ominous spin on the verdict that lay in store
for George.

CHAPTER 8

Trial, Prosecution

ASSISTANT DEFENSE ATTORNEY JOSEPH POWER ENTERED JUDGE FIN-
negan's courtroom at 9:30 a.m., on Wednesday morning. George, along
with Eleanor and Leo, were in "lockup"—in the guarded and secure area
of the courtroom set aside for prisoners. As Power approached the area,
George could see that despite his attorney's starched shirt and carefully
pressed black suit, he looked tired and worn. Power told George that he
would have to withdraw from the case, as his father had died the previous night and he had family matters to attend to, including his father's
funeral.

Instead of postponing the trial even a day or two, the judge substi-
tuted Frank J. Ferlic, another assistant public defender, in Power's place.
When Ferlic arrived in the courtroom, he addressed the gentlemen of the
jury and stated, "I certainly hope that you will indulge me this afternoon
and understand that I am in a peculiar position. I came into this case
yesterday morning, and all I can do is argue the evidence." (At a later date,
Attorney Ferlic claimed that he had, at least, sat in on one prior interview
with George, a claim George would deny.)

According to "People vs. George Dale" (a December 1933 appeal
before the Illinois Supreme Court), George, as "petitioner," suddenly was
without competent counsel, as was his right under Illinois law. As George
later stated:

*Your Petitioner further states that he is an ordinary layman; that
he is unfamiliar with Court procedure; that he was dismayed and*

astonished at this unusual turn of events; that he did not know what to do; that he thought it unfair and against every principle of justice known to the Courts of this State to be represented by counsel to whom he had not talked; to whom he had never told his story or his defense; and in whom he had no confidence as to his ability because he did not know him.

There had been some discussion in the chambers about continuing the trial until after Attorney Power's return, but Attorney Schultze (representing Eleanor) and Attorney Abrams (representing Leo) optimistically stated that their clients would take the witness stand and "tell the truth." Instead George, who was unprepared—as was his counsel—would end up testifying instead of Leo. For George, Attorney Ferlic's entrance into the trial did not bode well.

PROSECUTION PRESENTS ITS CASE

With George's new public defender in place, Prosecutor Wilbert Crowley immediately began to present his case for the People of the State of Illinois. By mid-afternoon, he called thirty-eight individuals to the witness stand. He also made a few opening statements, but the only one mentioned by the press was that the state had demanded the death penalty. Everyone, it seemed, was eager hear what the witnesses had to say.

The prosecution's first witness was Carrie Hoeh, Gustav's widow. Wearing a print dress and a black hat, she walked to the witness stand, raised her right hand, and swore to "tell the truth, the whole truth, and nothing but the truth." She explained that Gustav had been a sole proprietor, and that they had lived in an apartment behind the shop. He didn't own a gun, Carrie stated, and she never saw a gun in the shop. She testified that Gustav had been in good health. She managed to keep her composure when she added, "I last saw my husband at the chapel, after he was dead."

The second witness was Edwin D. Grant, the police officer who had been directing traffic near Gustav's shop. Officer Grant hadn't seen the shooting, but he was close enough to hear the commotion. He accompanied the dying man to the West Suburban Hospital in a truck belonging to the next witness, Theodore Nielsen.

WITNESSES

Then thirty-five more witnesses were called to testify for the prosecution. Those taking the stand included eyewitnesses at the scene of the crime, a ballistics expert, a deputy coroner, and the two sons of Gustav Hoeh, as well as crime scene investigators, other police officers, and detectives. Not all of the eyewitnesses agreed on what they claimed to have seen and heard, particularly as to the number of shots fired. Some said two, some three, and some four. Neither could they concur as to whether Eleanor had carried anything in her hand, or if she had physically struck the shopkeeper. Clearly, no witness said she had kicked the dying man in the face or groin, as some newspaper writers later reported.

After the widow, the police officer, and the truck driver, the next witnesses, in order of appearance were:

- Mae Swanson, shop owner
- William Frederick, shop customer
- Seth Wiard, ballistics expert
- Grover F. Mulvaney, deputy coroner

Mae Swanson, the first of the eyewitnesses, owned a tailor shop across the street from Hoeh's shop. As part of her testimony, she stated, "I saw Mr. Hoeh appear to be grappling with some man and sort of held him by what appeared to be his hand and neck, and there was a woman in back of him who seemed to be trying to break them loose." She then added, "This man broke loose and stepped back about four feet and fired a shot which hit Mr. Hoeh in the chest." She then pointed out George in the courtroom as the man who pulled the trigger.

The tailor shop owner then told the court that she had seen all three defendants at the "show-up" at the Austin Police Station on August 10. According to later testimony, spectators in the courtroom had been told that Captain Malone had called Mae Swanson and several of the other witnesses to the police station to ask whether they could identify Eleanor, George, and Leo. At that time, Leo had made several voluntary statements, distancing himself from Eleanor and George by repeatedly telling whoever would listen that he had been shot in the hand trying to prevent George from shooting Gustav Hoeh. He also was quick to tell everyone that George had announced, "This is a stick-up," a charge that George later denied.

On the witness stand and during cross-examination by Attorney Schultze about whether Eleanor may have struck the shopkeeper with or without a purse or sap in her hand, Mae Swanson responded, "I do not believe the woman [Eleanor] I saw there carried anything in her hand." Then, a few minutes later, she muddled her own testimony by stating, "I couldn't say whether she held anything in her hand from where I was standing."

The next witness was William Frederick, who had been a customer in a barber shop across the street at the time of the shooting. He saw "two men and a woman" struggling with the shopkeeper at the entrance to Hoeh's shop. Of the woman (Eleanor) he stated, "She was right on top of Mr. Hoeh, straddling over, striking him on the back. I did not see what she struck him with. I just noticed her fist. I did not see anything in her hand."

Following Frederick was the testimony of Seth Wiard, an associate in ballistics at the Scientific Crime Detection Laboratory of Northwestern University. He defined ballistics as "detecting and determining the relationship between fired bullets and guns." His first question came from the prosecutor who asked, "I show you some lead pellets [fired bullets], People's Exhibit No. 10, being one complete pellet [fired bullet] and two parts of another pellet [fired bullet], and ask you whether or not you have had occasion to examine those pellets [fired bullets] in connection with those arms?" After the witness examined them, the attorney explained to the court that the reason he introduced Seth Wiard as a witness was that he intended to trace the bullets to one of the guns and, thus, determine its owner.

Defense attorney Ferlic, on behalf of George, objected and said that a discussion of the guns would incriminate his client, but his objection was overruled. Attorney Ferlic then pointed out that no foundation had been laid for the topic of guns, and that their discussion was "highly improper and highly prejudicial." Nevertheless, ballistics expert Wiard was allowed to proceed. As he testified, "I fired two bullets for identification through People's Exhibit 6, [a .38 caliber Harrington & Richardson revolver] seized at the time of Eleanor's and George's arrests. After the bullets had been fired, there were marks left on those bullets, and from those marks I was able to make a comparative analysis of the test bullets and the bullets that were furnished me for investigation and examination."

Deputy coroner Grover F. Mulvaney was next on the witness stand. He testified that he took the bullets from the Cook County Coroner's Office to the Crime Detection Laboratory. (As to where they had been found, Officer Albert Glass later testified that the steel jacket of one bullet, as well as the mashed bullet, had been picked up by police at the crime scene and then sent, by police, to the Cook County Coroner's Office.) The physician who had examined Gustav Hoeh's body during his autopsy had not yet appeared in court, but the prosecutor spoke on his behalf and gave the results of the autopsy. He confirmed that one bullet had entered the man's heart, and another bullet had entered his liver, but both had exited his body.

MORE WITNESSES
Then came eight more eyewitnesses:

- Dorothy McFee, employee in a physician's office
- Vincent Homings, engraving shop owner
- George English, restaurant owner
- Leo Ensworth, patron in store across the street from Hoeh's shop
- Morris Zimbler, newsstand owner and restaurant patron
- Dominic Varraveto, pedestrian
- John Brabec and Estelle Rogers, passing motorists who chased getaway car

Dorothy McFee was working in a nearby physician's office. She testified that, from the office window, she saw a man shoot Gustav Hoeh. She claimed to have heard three shots and didn't see anything in the hands of "the girl." Then, when the man was pushing "the girl" into a car, McFee grabbed a piece of paper and wrote down the car's license plate number. She stated that she, like Mae Swanson, later identified Eleanor and George at the "show-up" at the Austin Police Station. She, too, was present for one of Leo's voluntary statements and remembered Leo saying that he only went into the shop to buy a shirt.

Testifying next was Vincent Homings, owner of an engraving shop next door to Gustav Hoeh's shop. "I watched a man with a gun in his hands as he was backing up to the machine [getaway car]," he stated. "I cannot recall that I saw him fire any shots. I do not remember how many shots were fired, but I know there was more than one." Like the previous witness, Vincent Homings wrote down the car's license plate number.

George English was at his restaurant, two doors west of Hoeh's, shop when he heard reports of the shooting from his wife who ran in and then fainted. By the time English got outside to see what was going on, he saw "two or three people scuffling" and heard another shot. Of the woman (Eleanor), he said she that did not have anything in her hand and specifically added, "I did not see her kick old man Hoeh while he was lying prostrate."

Leo Ensworth was a patron in a store across the street from Hoeh's shop. He heard three shots and ran outside to see what was going on. He saw Gustav Hoeh lying on the sidewalk and a man and a woman running toward a car. He said that the woman (Eleanor) did not have anything in her hand.

Next on the stand was Morris Zimbler, owner of two newsstands on opposite corners of Division Street. He had been sitting in a restaurant, heard two shots fired, and ran outside. He was one of the men who lifted Gustav Hoeh into Theodore Nielsen's truck and then jumped in and accompanied them (and Officer Grant as well) to the hospital. A pedestrian, Dominic Varraveto, was walking by Hoeh's shop when he heard "two or three" shots, then saw a man and a woman enter a car. He didn't remember if the woman had anything in her hand.

The following witnesses, John Brabec and Estelle Rogers, were in their own car at the time of the shooting. They had traveled north on Austin Boulevard and were stopped at a traffic light at Division Street just as the defendants sped away from the scene of the shooting. Brabec and Rogers saw the shopkeeper bleeding on the sidewalk and initially thought he was the victim of a hit-and-run driver, so they decided to chase the car. As Estelle Rogers testified, they caught up with the defendants at a traffic light and pulled up alongside of them. The driver (Leo) looked over and asked, "What's the matter?" while Estelle was writing down the license plate number. The couple then returned to Division Street to become the third party to give the plate number to the police who, by then, had arrived at the scene.

POLICE AND OTHERS

Then came police officers who, no doubt, had been told to read their police procedural manual that provided instructions while on the witness stand. As the manual's writer stated:

> *The witness is a salesman trying to convey to the court information which it will accept, and his success depends not only upon his knowledge but also upon the manner in which he gives his testimony and his conduct on the stand. Witnesses should be definite, fair, and frank, stating exactly what the facts are, without malice or favor to either side.*

Also written was advice on an officer's appearance and conduct in the courtroom. "Audible or energetic gum-chewing or toothpick gymnastics may amuse the members of the jury," the writer stated, "but do not raise their estimation of the performer."

In order of their testimonies, the law enforcement members were:

- Martin Wasberger, crime scene investigator
- John J. Collins, crime scene investigator
- Donald Coakley, detective who (with Dooley) arrested Leo
- Edward Dooley, detective who (with Coakley) arrested Leo

77

Figure 8.1. Here, Eleanor was photographed in the courtroom. She still wore her wedding ring, or perhaps she put it on for the trial. Chicago Tribune Historical Photos/TCA.

- William V. Blaul, chief of detectives
- Albert Glass, officer who arrested Eleanor and George
- Patrick C. Touhy, officer who assisted in arrests of Eleanor and George
- Willard L. Malone, captain of District 28, Austin Police Station

Martin Wasberger, a police officer in Captain Malone's 28th District, had been one of the first officers to arrive at the scene. Like crime scene investigators of today, Officer Wasberger examined the premises where he found one bullet and two pellets (fired bullets), as identified in People's Exhibit 10 in the ballistics expert's testimony. The officer said that the bullets were on the floor, "right at the door on the inside." He put his "mark" on them, explaining that, with his pocketknife, he made "a little scratch on the inside rim" so he could identify the bullets in court. Another police officer, John J. Collins, followed. He had arrived at the scene later in the afternoon and discovered that the glass in one of the showcases was broken. Inside the showcase, he found a "copper-colored bullet" and turned it over to Captain Malone. Oddly, it never was entered into evidence.

Following the crime scene investigators were the two detectives, Donald Coakley and Edward Dooley. They were the men who had stayed with Leo's wife at his apartment, and Officer Dooley was the officer who had talked with Leo on the phone and convinced him to turn himself in. After detectives Coakley and Dooley had arrested Leo, they took him to the Detective Bureau to be questioned by Chicago's Chief of Detectives, William V. Blaul. Chief Blaul was next on the witness stand and confirmed that Leo gave a statement in his presence.

The prosecutor then asked the judge if he could read Leo's previous statement to the jury, but George's counsel, as well as assistant defense attorney Ferlic and Attorney Schultze (on behalf of Eleanor), objected. Judge Finnegan asked the jury to leave the courtroom while the attorneys decided how to proceed. Their concern was that the statement also named Eleanor and George. For a courtroom reading of the statement, the prosecutor agreed to substitute "a man" in place of George's name and "a lady or a woman" in place of Eleanor's. Leo's statement then was read and entered into evidence as "People's Exhibit 14." Then Chief Blaul got back on the stand. In addition to being present for questioning after Leo's arrest, he confirmed that he had been present after Eleanor's and George's arrests, as well.

Officer Albert Glass, of the 28th District, was next and testified that he had assisted in the arrests of Eleanor and George on Drexel Avenue.

The first question asked of him by the prosecutor was, "At the time you got in there, did you see any guns?" Attorney Ferlic, representing George, interjected the popular courtroom refrain, declaring that the question was "improper, immaterial, and irrelevant." As expected, Judge Finnegan overruled the objection.

Officer Glass continued his testimony and stated that he had found guns "wrapped in a bundle, tied with a string or cord, on the floor under the bed." During cross-examination, Attorney Schultze asked Officer Glass if he had obtained a search warrant "to make a search of the premises." After Officer Glass responded, "no," the prosecutor interjected and stated, "He doesn't need warrants." The prosecutor also claimed that no search warrants had been needed, either, for Eleanor's and/or George's arrests.

Attorney Schultze continued his cross-examination by asking the officer, "How did you know where to go, where the defendants lived?" Without elaborating, Officer Glass answered, "We had information that they were there." The informant's name, Richard Slater (Eleanor's former boyfriend), however, was kept out of the officer's testimony. Richard wasn't even asked to testify. Nor was Leo's wife, Tina. Legally, she didn't have to testify against her husband, but she could have been put on the stand and asked about Eleanor and George.

Assisting in the arrests of Eleanor and George was Officer Patrick C. Touhy. He confirmed Officer Glass's testimony, as well as the dates and times that Eleanor, George, and Leo were questioned at the Austin Police Station. To wrap up the law enforcement testimony, Captain Willard L. Malone took the stand and stated that he had served as a police officer for thirty-four years. He, too, confirmed his presence during the questioning of the defendants. Of Leo and his voluntary statements, Captain Malone stated, "I heard the defendant [Leo] Minneci make statements—eight different times—in reference to the shooting of Mr. Hoeh. They were made in the presence of people who came there to look at Mr. Minneci and these other defendants."

CONCLUDING THE PROSECUTION'S CASE

The prosecution continued its presentation with Gustav's sons, Earl and Norman, as well as Herbert Eide, a family friend. Norman said that he, too, had been present for all eight of Leo's statements. Earl testified that he occasionally had helped his father in the store, and, to his knowledge, Gustav never owned a gun. Then the prosecutor said he would introduce into evidence the four revolvers [People's Exhibits 6, 7, 8, and 9] found in the rented room at the time of Eleanor's and George's arrests. Attorney Ferlic objected, stating that the prosecution had not shown that the guns were in the exclusive possession of the defendants. Ferlic further stated that he still did not believe the prosecution had laid the proper foundation to introduce the guns into evidence.

Judge Finnegan agreed with Attorney Ferlic's objection and asked the jury to leave the courtroom so the attorneys could approach the bench. Ferlic extended his objection of the guns to an objection of the bullets, and Eleanor's and Leo's attorneys agreed. The prosecutor then said that the testimony of the ballistics expert had confirmed which gun had fired the fatal bullet, but Ferlic correctly pointed out, "I don't believe he has told us whether that gun (which was used at the time of the murder) was in this particular package or not." The judge overruled Ferlic's objection.

After the jury returned, the prosecutor proceeded to enter the guns into evidence. He also offered into evidence the "three pellets [fired bullets], being the evidence bullets recovered at the scene in Mr. Hoeh's store." They were followed with the entry of the "two pellets [fired bullets] used by the ballistics expert for the purpose of comparative analysis." The prosecution also entered into evidence two notations of the getaway car's license plate number, as well as the voluntary statements that Eleanor, George, and Leo had made to the police and in the presence of each other.

After the prosecutor had finished reading the statements, he announced that Dr. Thomas L. Dwyer (the physician who had performed the autopsy) was not able to attend the trial. In his place, the prosecutor read a statement that confirmed that the cause of Hoeh's death was a result of "gunshot wounds of the chest, hemorrhage, and shock." Jury members were shown autopsy photographs that then were entered into evidence as People's Exhibits 2, 3, 4, and 5. Another physician, Dr. Harry R. Hoffman, then testified, briefly, to make a slight correction, as to wording, in the autopsy report.

ROBBERY VICTIMS

Finally, the prosecution brought in the ten daylight victims: F. E. Georgeson, Myron Schaeffer, Cornelius J. Lutterman, Joseph F. Hrejsa, J. W. Nosarzewski, Grace Rutledge, Benjamin Lack (sometimes spelled Lock), James Swoik, A. C. Mell, and Anna Soll, as well as Elva Denning. None, however, were permitted to speak about their robberies, as prior crimes of the defendants were inadmissible during the trial. The prosecutor started with F. E. Georgeson, who identified herself as an employee of the Mayfield Dry Goods store. The questioning proceeded as follows:

> Prosecutor: "I show you Jarman, the defendant, Dale, the defendant, and Minneci, the defendant. Did you ever see those three together before?"
>
> Georgeson: "Yes."
>
> Crowley: "Where?"
>
> Georgeson: "Mayfield Dry Goods, June 28th."
>
> Crowley: "What time?"
>
> Georgeson: "2:15 p.m."

Then, at defense attorney Ferlic's request, the jury left the room. Ferlic asked the prosecutor what he was trying to prove with this line of questioning. The prosecutor replied, "I am proving association between the three defendants." As expected, Ferlic's reply was, "irrelevant and immaterial." After the jury returned, the same questions were asked of each of the other robbery victims. Each time, the defense attorneys objected, and each time they were overruled.

After the last victim's testimony, the prosecution rested its case.

CHAPTER 9

Trial, Defense

THE PROSECUTION HAD CALLED THIRTY-EIGHT WITNESSES TO THE stand, but the defense only had two—George and Eleanor. On Wednesday, August 30, both would try to shift the blame to Leo, who, on the advice of counsel, did not testify as originally planned. The prosecutor would come back, though, with a big punch by using one of the robbery victims as a rebuttal witness.

GEORGE TAKES THE STAND

George's testimony was first. Before being questioned, he spoke of his background, but much of what he swore to, under oath, was incorrect. According to the press, none of his family was in the courtroom. His mother was deceased, but George likely was trying to protect his father and siblings from being preyed upon by reporters. Without Internet resources to personal information that reporters and investigators have at their fingertips today, no one knew whether George was telling the truth. According to the December 1933 Illinois Supreme Court documents, his testimony began:

> *My name is George Dale. At the time I was arrested, I was living at 6323 Drexel. I am 28 years old. I was born in St. Louis. I lived in St. Louis about eight or nine years prior to coming to Chicago. I moved to Chicago from St. Louis. My father has been dead since about 1918. My mother has been dead since 1917. I have no brothers or sisters.*

George was correct in saying that his mother was deceased, but his father, John M. Dale, was alive and well in Fredericktown, Madison County, Missouri, nearly one hundred miles south of St. Louis. John Dale was the sole proprietor of a shop (as had been murder victim Gustav Hoeh) in Fredericktown, the community where George and his siblings were born and raised. (They were not from St. Louis as George had claimed.) Three brothers had died in childhood, but George's five remaining siblings were alive at the time of George's trial. His sister Margaret (with whom he lived in 1930) was still living in Chicago; Julia and Lucille were in Arkansas; Eugene was in Poplar Bluff, Missouri; and Walter was in San Antonio, Texas. According to federal census records, George was born in 1903, making him twenty-nine or thirty years old.

In George's version of the murder, he stated that he, Eleanor, and Leo went into Hoeh's store to buy a shirt, but Hoeh didn't have George's size. His account of the shooting, in part, was as follows:

I went over and stepped over to [Leo] Minneci and looked at what he was looking at and there was some kind of argument began about the shirts. I don't know, we got to scuffling around there, the first thing I know, a gun shot was fired, I do not know who by, and we all three—Mrs. [Eleanor] Jarman did not have anything to do with this at all, she was there looking at ties, and when she heard the shot fired, she went out. We three, [Leo] Minneci and I and Mr. Hoeh. I did not have a gun with me. I really do not know if Mr. Hoeh had a gun. I can't say that Leo Minneci had a gun. Mrs. Jarman did not have a gun that I know of. Not at any time that I know of did I see Mr. Hoeh have a gun in the store. Something was said about shirts. He was looking at shirts on that side. The argument did not last very long, maybe about three or four minutes. I really do not know what Mr. Hoeh did. We got in an argument and a scuffle and that was all there was to that.

I did not at any time tell Mr. Hoeh, "Stick them up" [as Leo had previously stated]. I did not go in that store for the purpose of holding up Mr. Hoeh. I went there only for the purpose of buying shirts, and there was an argument. After we left the store, we got in the car and drove away. We drove west on Division, turned north and then west, and came back south. Not that I know of did anyone go to the cash register in Mr. Gustav Hoeh's store. Not to my knowledge was any money taken from Mr. Hoeh. I do not know if any attempt was made to take any money from Mr. Hoeh. I am absolutely positive of that.

On cross-examination, Prosecutor Crowley managed to get George to give more details of previous relationships and events, some of which may have been correct. George said that he thought he had met Eleanor in January 1933, adding that they had lived together part of the time. He also stated that on August 4, he, Eleanor, and Leo rode around in Leo's brother's car from 1:00 p.m. to 2:40 p.m. "We frequently went to the North Side and took a ride around the boulevard system," he stated. During that time, they stopped at a gas station where he bought some gasoline.

Of the gun (People's Exhibit 6) that the ballistics expert testified was used in the shooting, George insisted that it was not his and stated:

The police officers may have gotten it out of the room at the time I was arrested, yes. I don't know that they did get it out of my room. They said they got this gun, too, out of my room. That is what they said. I was there at the time. I did not see them get these guns. I do not know how they got the guns out of there. They were wrapped up, according to them. They were wrapped up according to the police, yes. [Eleanor] Jarman did not wrap them up. We were not going to ditch them.

The prosecutor continued to question George about guns. Then the prosecutor brought in robbery victim James Swoik.

Prosecutor: "Now, on August 4, 1933, did you or not have a gun?"

George: "I did not."

Prosecutor: "Mr. Swoik, stand up. Mr. Swoik, stand up here. Take a look at this man. Let the record show Mr. Swoik is standing up."

Defense Attorney Frank J. Ferlic: "If the court please, I object."

Prosecutor: "Let me finish my question. On August 4, 1933, at 4050 West North Avenue, in the presence of this man, did you have a gun in your possession?"

George: "I did not."

Defense Attorney Ferlic: "I object, your Honor, it is highly improper and highly prejudicial."

The Court: "Overruled."

By introducing James Swoik during George's testimony, the prosecution had laid the foundation for his further questioning at the conclusion of the trial.

ELEANOR'S TESTIMONY

After George's testimony, it was Eleanor's turn to take the stand. A *Chicago Tribune* reporter who preferred sensationalism over accuracy noted her appearance and wrote, "Mrs. Jarman, whose blonde [*sic*] hair was somewhat disarrayed, wept—for sympathy, the prosecutor would later say in his closing argument—when she took the witness stand. As the tears rolled down her cheeks, she dabbed her face with a blue-bordered handkerchief." An *Associated Press* article, distributed all over the country, stated that Eleanor "broke down while recounting her life story," adding that "economic necessity had forced her into a career of banditry."

Although the spectators in the courtroom didn't know the difference, Eleanor, like George, fabricated some of her personal history. Her personal statement, published by the Supreme Court of the State of Illinois, December Term A.D. 1933 as *The People of the State of Illinois vs. George Dale, otherwise known as George Kennedy; Eleanor Jarman, and Leo Minneci*, began:

> *My name is Eleanor Jarman. Before I was arrested, I lived at 4300 West Madison. I am 29 years old. I am married but separated and not divorced. I do not know if I was born in Iowa or California. I really do not know which. My mother died when I was young. I was about 6 years old when my mother died. My father is not living. He is also*

dead. I do not really remember how old I was when he died, but he died a few years after my mother.

Woodbury County, Iowa, birth records clearly show that Eleanor, as "Ella Berendt," was born in Sioux City, Iowa, on April 22, 1901. At the time of her testimony, she was thirty-two years old, not twenty-nine. She was correct in saying that she had been six years old when her mother died, but she was eighteen years old (quite a bit older) when her father passed away. Eleanor then mentioned that she had two sons, "Leon and Lebrun." Their correct names, however, were LeRoy and LaVerne.

As to her work history, Eleanor apparently told the truth. After she separated from her husband, she "went right to work," adding:

I was doing waitress work. I worked at first two or three different places, or several places rather, until I got used to the work. And then I worked at different places. Some places I worked a year and some two years and another place I worked three years. I worked at a restaurant on Madison and Kedzie for three years or better. I quit about nine or ten months ago. I worked some since then but not much. I was working for a friend of mine. He had a girl more or less to answer the telephone. His business wasn't so good, and he didn't have steady girls, and now and then I would work for him and take his phone calls.

I have been unemployed for about nine months, outside of those few days I answered the phone for this friend of mine. I had to go to the Charities for help during the time I was unemployed. The Charities helped me about three months. Then they told me to notify them if I got a job. I took two weeks work answering this phone again, and they stopped my charity entirely. I really couldn't say what month I met Mr. [George] Dale. But it was last winter sometime. I know [Leo] Minneci about the same length of time.

Under cross-examination from the prosecutor, Eleanor was more specific about her "friend," as well as to how she paid her rent. "The money for the rent—well, I was working for a short while, and [George] Dale helped me," she testified. "[But] he did not always give me the money for the rent. The name of the gentleman for whom I answered telephones is Slater. He is more or less a pretty good friend of mine."

MORE TESTIMONY IN THE PRESS

On August 31, reporter George Wright of the *Chicago Tribune* published a portion of Eleanor's direct examination by her attorney, A. Jefferson Schultze, as follows:

Attorney Schultze: "Did anyone have a gun in the store that you know of?"

Eleanor: "No."

Attorney Schultze: "Did you stop on the sidewalk and hit Hoeh?"

Eleanor: "No."

Attorney Schultze: "Did you strike him on the head?"

Eleanor: "No."

Attorney Schultze: "Did you claw at him?"

Eleanor: "No."

Then Prosecutor Crowley began his cross-examination.

Prosecutor Crowley: "When you slugged the old man, you were thinking of protecting your boy chum, Dale, or Kennedy, as you call him. Isn't that right?"

Eleanor: "No. I didn't hit him."

Prosecutor Crowley: "If you were not hiding and running away from a crime you knew was committed, why didn't you go to the police?"

Eleanor: "I had my children to think of."

Prosecutor Crowley: "Didn't you, as a matter of fact, have a gun a half hour before the murder?"

Eleanor: "No."

Crowley: "Did [George] Dale?"

Eleanor: "No."

SWOIK, THE REBUTTAL WITNESS

Eleanor's last answer, testifying that George did *not* have a gun, gave the prosecutor an opportunity to again question James Swoik. As a rebuttal witness, Swoik could rebut, or invalidate, previous testimony. This time he was able to confirm that he had seen the three defendants in his store thirty minutes before the Hoeh murder, and that George did have a revolver at that time.

Swoik's testimony, as published in the Supreme Court document of December 1933, read as follows:

James Swoik: "My name is James Swoik. I am the same James Swoik who testified earlier this morning."

Prosecutor Crowley: "Calling your attention to the 4th day of August 1933, at 2 p.m., did you see the three defendants at your store at 4050 North Avenue in Chicago, Cook County, Illinois?"

James Swoik: "I did."

Attorney Schultze: "I object to the question."

The Court: "Overruled."

Schultze: "Similar ground as stated an hour ago."

Prosecutor: "Did you see them there?"

James Swoik: "Yes, sir."

Prosecutor: "Did you see any gun at the time you saw them there?"

James Swoik: "I did."

Prosecutor: "Who had the gun?"

James Swoik: "[George] Dale."

Prosecutor: "Will you point out the [George] Dale that you are referring to as having the gun?"

Attorney Ferlic: "If the court please, I wish to object to the question and the testimony given here on the ground the Supreme Court has many times held on the question of other offenses, it is highly incompetent and highly prejudicial."

The Court: "Objection overruled."

Ferlic: "Exception."

After Swoik's testimony was concluded, he "indicated [pointed out] the defendant Dale, also known as Kennedy."

CLOSING AND VERDICT

In the afternoon, in front of a packed courtroom, Prosecutor Crowley gave his closing statements. Speaking directly to the jury and still not mentioning that James Swoik and the other victims had been robbed, the prosecutor emphasized the importance of the other robbery victims' earlier statements and Swoik's recent testimony. The prosecutor unequivocally stated:

Figure 9.1. In this courtroom scene, Eleanor stood between her attorney, A. Jefferson Schultze, and codefendant Leo Minneci. On the right is George Dale. Chicago Tribune Historical Photos/TCA.

[George] Dale says he didn't have a gun. He had it half an hour earlier in another man's store, and the other two were with him. They said they didn't know anything about a gun. They knew it half an hour before, and they were associates together. Don't you remember? Eleven people told you this morning about those people being associated together. Two out of the eleven said [Eleanor] Jarman and [Leo] Minneci were associated on two different occasions, and in the rest of them all three of them were associated together.

In reference to Eleanor, and pushing for the death penalty, the prosecutor was even more emphatic:

What strange law it is, in this present day that permits a woman by pretentious tears to cause men to hesitate about treating her with the same sort of justice that they mete out to their fellow men? I say to you men in this case, don't give [George] Dale any more than you give her. She is just as guilty as he. Oh, her buddies, her gang, her pals. She is a killer.

When the jury retired to the jury room, the spectators held their seats—for four hours and eleven minutes. The jury's first duty was to select one of them as a foreman to preside over their deliberations. The men returned at 9:30 p.m., but the judge made everyone wait for fifteen long minutes before the foreman was permitted to read the verdict. No one knew what was going on at the time, but a newspaper reporter later explained that Leo, waiting in a detention room, "acted like a madman when he was informed that the jury had decided on a verdict. It took bailiffs fifteen minutes to quiet him sufficiently to bring him into the courtroom." As the reporter continued, "He [Leo] had clawed helplessly at the bars both before and after the verdict was read."

Leo was guarded by four bailiffs when he was returned to the courtroom. Other bailiffs were scattered throughout the room with orders from the judge to maintain quiet. Even so, several women (believed to have been Leo's wife and Leo's mother) screamed, as the foreman read

Leo's verdict—199 years in the state penitentiary. All three defendants, though, appeared relieved that Leo had not received the death penalty.

"Then," stated the *Tribune*'s reporter, "the [199-year] verdict on Mrs. [Eleanor] Jarman was read. She could be heard to sigh with relief that she, too, had escaped the electric chair. [George] Dale seemed encouraged, but only for a moment. He slumped in his chair when the clerk read the jury's verdict fixing the death penalty for him. It was Dale who fired the shot that killed Hoeh."

None of George's nor Eleanor's family were in the courtroom. After the verdicts, the attorneys for all three defendants entered motions for new trials. By then, it was late in the evening, so the motions, as well as formal sentencing, were continued to September 1. As the crowd began to leave, one of Gustav Hoeh's sons, Earl, speaking for the family, told a reporter that they were "satisfied" with the verdict. "The verdict is very fair," he said. "Mrs. [Eleanor] Jarman and [Leo] Minneci will virtually be buried alive in the penitentiary."

The reporter then tried, unsuccessfully, to get a comment from Eleanor but he ended up writing, "She could only moan 'Get away, get away,' as she sat in the court detention room, tears streaming down her cheeks."

Figure 9.2. The *Chicago Tribune* titled this after-verdict photograph "'Tiger' and Co-Defendants Guilty, Dale gets Death, Mrs. Jarman and Minneci 199 Years." Captain Malone is out of view, but his star badge is visible on the left. Chicago Tribune Historical Photos/TCA.

PART III

BEHIND BARS, 1933–1940

CHAPTER 10

One-Way Ticket

IN A POSTTRIAL INTERVIEW WITH THE PRESS, THE JURORS STATED THAT they had no arguments as to the guilt of any of the defendants. The "terrible fight," as some of them later described a heated discussion in the jury room, was over the punishments for Eleanor and Leo. Their sentences of 199 years, a record in Cook County, had been a compromise between jurors who wanted to execute all three defendants and those who hesitated to inflict death on a woman. Instead they wanted to guarantee that neither Eleanor nor Leo ever would ever go free. At the time, a parole law required that a defendant had to serve at least one-third of his or her sentence, so the 199-year penalties would ensure that both defendants would be in their nineties before they could get out of prison. Or so the jurors thought, at the time.

Prosecutor Crowley was satisfied with the verdict, even though he had asked for the death penalty not only for George, but for Leo and Eleanor as well. The sentences, he emphasized, were meant as deterrents. "This verdict," he stated, "along with the others which have recently been rendered by courageous jurors, should strike terror in the hearts of the criminal element."

STILL NEWSWORTHY

Meanwhile, most of the reporters covering Eleanor continued to push the "blonde tigress" narrative. A *Chicago Tribune* reporter wrote, "Some of the witnesses even said she [Eleanor] kicked Hoeh while he was on the sidewalk bleeding to death from the wound inflicted by Dale."

Another with slightly different wording stated, "Mrs. [Eleanor] Jarman was accused of having kicked the aged murder victim in the face as he lay dying." These and other accusations were made solely by the press. There was *no* mention in the eyewitness testimonies of Eleanor kicking anyone, but sensationalism continued to sell newspapers.

One editorial writer who perpetuated the kicking (and even clawing) account differed, however, on the use of the "blonde tigress" moniker. It may have been, as the writer stated, initially used by the police, but the *Chicago Tribune*, followed by other newspapers, fanned the flames. The editor's short piece, published on August 31, 1933, in the *Lincoln Star*, in Lincoln, Nebraska (where Eleanor and Michael LeRoy Jarman married), read as follows:

> *Some ingenious Chicago policeman coined the name "Blonde Tigress," when thirty-year-old Mrs. Eleanor Jarman was accused of participation in a particularly atrocious murder. With Chicago's anti-crime drive pushing forward with full speed, Mrs. Jarman, mother of two children, was sentenced to 199 years captivity.*
>
> *The police unthinkingly are defeating their own purposes in christening Mrs. Jarman as a "Blonde Tigress." It casts a glamor about her undeserved. Her pictures reveal a very ordinary looking woman. Her record discloses an element of brutality and cruelty and depravity that needs to be called by the exact words which describe it.*
>
> *There is altogether too much tendency to lift ruthless criminals into an unreal, extraordinary position. They are merely human beings who have gone wrong, and when caught and punished as Mrs. Jarman was, they become, in fact, a rather pathetic figure. They are not entitled to sympathy nor to exploitation. They should be seen as they are—ignorant, lawless, to be scorned by decent-thinking people.*

After the verdict, the defendants' attorneys needed a day to get their paperwork in order prior to formal sentencing. As a result, there were no court proceedings on Thursday, August 31. Eleanor, George, and Leo remained in their cells at the Cook County Jail. Someone, perhaps a *Chicago Tribune* photographer, arranged for Eleanor to shed her prison clothes for a fancy dress. He posed her looking through the bars on the window of her cell and clutching a handkerchief.

The *Chicago Tribune* reporter described Eleanor as "calm," stating that "she appeared to have dropped five years off of her age since the conviction." He then added that "lines of worry had disappeared, and the tenseness was gone from her husky voice." Eleanor told the reporter that for the first time after her arrest, she slept soundly. She called her 199-year sentence "a relief, as opposed to being sentenced to the electric chair." As to her crimes, Eleanor told the reporter, "There was nothing in it anyway but a lot of excitement and worry. I decided to go out and look for a job, but then I was arrested." When asked about her husband (Michael Roy Jarman), she said she "doesn't know or care where he is."

The same reporter apparently had tried to obtain interviews with George and Leo. George refused to see anyone, and Leo was said to be "muttering to himself." When Eleanor heard that Leo was "acting strangely," her reply was, "He's just putting that on to try to make an insanity plea. I've known him long enough to know that."

FORMAL SENTENCING

Friday, September 1, 1933, was the last day that that Eleanor, George, and Leo were transported, together, from their cells to the Cook County Courthouse. Word of their convictions had quickly spread across the country. But the trial wasn't officially over, as there still were procedures that Judge Phillip L. Finnegan needed to do to wrap up his case. One was to "strike off" Eleanor's, George's, and Leo's six robbery charges. According to a Chicago Crime Commission report, there was no need for the prosecutor to reinstate any of these indictments (including the robbery of James Swoik's store), as the testimonies that the defendants had been seen together had served their purpose of showing association among the defendants.

Then came formal sentencing. Eleanor, sobbing again, was the first to stand before Judge Finnegan. According to the *Chicago Tribune*'s story on September 2, 1933, she was taken into the courtroom where the judge asked if she had anything to say as to why her sentence should not be imposed. "I am innocent," Eleanor said. "I had no idea what the others

Figure 10.1. A newspaper photographer posed Eleanor in dress clothes in the Cook County Jail. Chicago Tribune Historical Photos/TCA.

were doing. It was just a chance acquaintance. Give me another chance."
The judge then asked, "Is that all?" When Eleanor said, "yes," the judge
replied, "I then sentence you to serve 199 years in the penitentiary. Take
her away and bring in [Leo] Minneci."

"[Leo] Minneci fingered a rosary when he was brought forward,"
wrote a reporter. "He started to make a plea for a new trial, frequently
referring to the judge as 'Father.' He said something about his three children. The judge replied curtly that he should have thought of them a long
time before." Then the writer recorded the following exchange:

> *"Well, I'll tell you," said the judge. "I will give you a new trial on one
> condition."*
>
> *Minneci, who had appeared to be trying to simulate insanity at
> various times since the jury found him guilty on Wednesday night,
> started to smile as the judge hesitated. His smile disappeared as the
> judge continued, "That is, that you plead guilty and submit to a bench
> trial (trial by judge without a jury). Then I will send you to the chair."*

George then was called forward to hear his death sentence. He spoke
up and stated, "There is something your honor should know. There was
another woman in this case. It wasn't Mrs. [Eleanor] Jarman who was in
the store. She was in the car outside. The woman's name is Mary Davis,
and she is the same size and description as Mrs. [Eleanor] Jarman."
When the judge asked Mary's whereabouts, George said he "could not
tell." Was this a last-ditch effort on George's part to absolve Eleanor from
her sentence? It seems likely that George made the comment without the
advice of counsel.

Judge Finnegan then read George his sentence. In part, he stated
that George was "guilty of said crime of murder in manner and form as
charged in the indictment . . . and, that he be taken from the bar of this
court to the Common Jail of Cook County from whence he came and
be confined in said jail in safe and secure custody until the thirteenth day
of October, A.D. 1933." The date would change, as he would appeal his
case to the Illinois Supreme Court, but his sentence stipulated that he
would be "put to death by having caused to pass through the body of said

defendant, George Dale, otherwise called George Kennedy, a current of electricity of sufficient intensity to cause death, and the application and continuance of such current through the body of said defendant until such defendant is dead."

Both of George's public defenders, Joseph P. Power and Frank J. Ferlic, signed and filed affidavits to vacate judgment (that is, to set aside the sentence) for George, who also signed a petition on his own behalf. George's petition included, "Your petitioner further represents that because of the lack of representation by counsel fully prepared to defend him, he failed to receive a fair trial, and because of this reason he feels that the jury found him guilty and sentenced him to death." Judge Finnegan, however, overruled the defense team's efforts and dismissed all motions, at the time, for a new trial.

When Eleanor, George, and Leo returned to the Cook County Jail after their formal sentencing, they no longer were notorious criminals but, simply, convicted felons. A headline in the September 1, 1933, edition of the *Sioux City Journal* read, "Two Children of Convicted Killer Are Living Here." A reporter who, no doubt, lacked concern for the privacy of Eleanor's children wrote, "Somewhere in Sioux City are two boys, one LeRoy, 11, and LaVerne, 9, sons of Mrs. Eleanor Jarman, convicted of murder and sentenced to 199 years in prison in Chicago Wednesday night." Then, in error as to the date that the boys arrived, the article continued, "The boys were placed in the home of Mrs. Jarman's sister, whose name she would not reveal, on the night of August 4, the night of the murder in Chicago of which Mrs. Jarman was convicted. In refusing to reveal the name of her sister, Mrs. Jarman said, 'I only hope the boys never learn about me.'"

A TRAIN RIDE

Back in jail, Eleanor was ordered by a jail matron to "pack up and be ready" to travel to the Oakdale Reformatory for Women. As the only women's correctional institution in Illinois, it was located between Chicago and Springfield in the town of Dwight. Another reporter, hovering over Eleanor in her jail cell, overheard the matron tell Eleanor, "I guess you will be going to your permanent home in the morning." Eleanor, the reporter noted, was "moody." Meanwhile, Leo packed his things to go to the Joliet Correctional Center, the men's state penitentiary, in Joliet, Illinois. George would stay in the Cook County Jail until his execution.

The next day, Saturday, September 2, a crowd of three hundred people gathered at the Chicago & Alton Railroad Station, at 37th Street and South California Avenue (one mile south of the jail), to watch Eleanor and the four other recently convicted women board the train that would take them out of Chicago. The *Tribune's* photographer stalked Eleanor as she was being escorted by a police matron and snapped several photos on the train platform. Eleanor wore the same blouse, skirt, and shoes that she had worn in court.

Also standing on the train platform, presumably to see her off, was a man who bore a strong resemblance to Eleanor's former boyfriend, Richard Slater (see figure 10.2). He kept a low profile, due, no doubt, to connections with the underworld. According to the *Chicago Tribune*, after the death of gangster Jack Zuta in 1930, Richard was publicly identified (but not arrested) as one of Zuta's "collectors," traveling from one illegal gambling house to another and handling gambling proceeds from illegal slot machines.

In Eleanor's hand, she clutched an "Amos 'n' Andy" candy box. Perhaps Richard had given it to her, or the box simply may have been a keepsake of happier times when she and her boys had listened to the popular radio shows.

The *Tribune's* reporter described the four other women convicts as follows:

- "Mrs. Bessie Opas, the wife with the flashy gold tooth, who is to serve a 1-to-15-year sentence for conspiring to murder her husband. She also was fined $2,000."

- "Mrs. Vera Carl, 37 years old, who has 14 years to serve for plotting the murder of her husband to collect his insurance. Carl was a grocer."

Figure 10.2. On September 2, 1933, a police matron escorted Eleanor onto a train in Chicago. The man on the left is believed to be Eleanor's friend Richard Slater. Compare the man's facial features, hat, and glasses to Richard's photo (figure 17.2) in chapter 17. DN-A-2409 Chicago Sun Times/Chicago Daily News collection, Chicago History Museum.

- "Mrs. Louise Murphy, 50 years old, who has a 20-year murder sentence to serve. She was convicted of slaying her common-law husband, William Grother."
- "Miss Katherine Brockman, 23 years old, of St. Louis, who is to serve a 1-to-10-year sentence for robbery. She acted as the lure for two bandits."

The reporter talked with the convicted women before they left the jail and wrote, "The women all primped as if they were going visiting, as they prepared in the jail for the ride to the prison. Mrs. [Eleanor] Jarman tried to keep up her spirits but obviously was upset. She started to weep several times, while Mrs. Opas and Mrs. Murphy tried to cheer her." Then, quoting Eleanor, the reporter stated, "All I've got to say is that I

Figure 10.3. Another photo on the train platform shows Eleanor talking with a photographer. The man on the left holding his hat to his face is a prisoner (along with Leo) being taken to the Joliet Correctional Center. DN-A-2403, Chicago Sun Times/ Chicago Daily News collection, Chicago History Museum.

was innocent of that last 'rap.' I do not think I deserved such a severe jolt. I was in on the other robberies with the men, but I didn't know that the Hoeh affair was to be a robbery."

According to the *Chicago Tribune* article, Mrs. Carl also seemed to be hard hit by her sentence. "Fourteen years is a long time, but I have a chance to be out in eight years," she said. "My son will be a grown man by that time, and I will have a lot to live for. I expect to get out in two or three years. I'm going to be a good girl in jail, and I expect my husband [whose murder she 'plotted'] will relent after a short time and help me. I think he will pay my fine for me."

Oddly, the reporter made no mention of the vast difference between Eleanor's 199-year sentence for being present during Hoeh's murder and Louise Murphy's sentence of twenty years for actually committing a murder. Nor was the reporter interested in Leo. He and another male prisoner climbed aboard the same train, then it steamed out of the station and headed southwest. A half hour later, at the "state prison" stop, guards escorted Leo and the other male prisoner off the train. Eleanor had a glimpse of the large and forbidding institution. By 1933, the year she was off to Oakdale, most of Joliet's incarcerated female inmates already had been transferred to the new women's reformatory.

As Chicago and the city of Joliet were left behind, the flat prairie land evolved into a landscape of towns, villages, and corn fields. The train continued through Elwood, Wilmington, Braidwood, Braceville, and Gardner before reaching Dwight. The small town had a population of 2,534 at the time of the 1930 federal census. According to the *Dwight Star and Herald*, "between 100 and 200" residents turned out to see Eleanor, "the famous prisoner," get off the 10:56 a.m. train. Eleanor, the four others, and one or two reporters immediately were ushered onto a bus for the short drive to the Oakdale Reformatory.

The *Chicago Tribune* reporter, however, hadn't been permitted to accompany the prisoners, but he added, in the newspaper article, "The women prisoners who, according to deputy sheriffs, seemed to enjoy the train ride, all started to weep simultaneously when the end of the journey was reached." If they were expecting a prison that looked like Joliet, however, they were in for a surprise. By 11:15 a.m., the women saw, in the distance, a cluster of brick and stone buildings set among oak and spruce trees on a 160-acre tract of farmland and forest. The automobile driver made a right turn, drove through an open gate, and stopped at the largest of the buildings.

One of the reporters who did manage to ride both the train and the bus with the women noted that one of them said, "If I'd a-known the joint was like this, I would have shot that bum ten years ago." Eleanor, however, likely was anxious and afraid, feeling very much alone.

CHAPTER 11

Oakdale Reformatory

ELEANOR BRACED HERSELF FOR IMPERSONAL SURROUNDINGS AND clanging steel doors, but she and the other new inmates soon found themselves in a room with tasteful and homey furnishings, almost like a well-to-do family's living room. A middle-aged woman waited in a hallway to usher them to the Identification Office where another staff member smiled, greeted each woman by name, and then assigned each one their inmate numbers. From then on, Eleanor became number 692. Her only photographs were mug shots—one full face and one profile.

After the other inmates had their mug shots taken and each had their fingers inked for fingerprints, they changed into prison-issued dresses and handed over their street clothes and shoes to be returned upon their release. With Eleanor's 199-year sentence, she knew she would never see her belongings again. Eleanor likely had a lot of questions, including: When would she be locked up? What would her cell be like? Would she have a cell mate? Would she be able to look out of a window?

Eleanor wouldn't get her questions answered that day. Oakdale Reformatory's intake procedures included family and work histories, as well as physical descriptions. Eleanor, at the time, measured five feet tall and weighed 110 pounds. Her description included "a slight build, blonde hair, and grey eyes." Her parents, she stated, were from Germany, and the family were Lutherans. In the words of the reformatory's staff member, Eleanor's economic condition was "marginal," and the motive for her crime was "desire for gain." Eleanor told the clerk that she smoked, but she didn't chew tobacco or drink alcoholic beverages.

Following the paperwork, Eleanor and the other inmates were taken to the institution's hospital, located within its newest building, a residence hall. Like any new inmate, Eleanor and the others were required to quarantine for two weeks. During that time, they were told, they would be examined by physicians, a dentist, and a psychiatrist—all women. The inmates would be asked if they were pregnant and would undergo screening for venereal and contagious diseases. It's not known if they were in seclusion, or if they could visit among themselves. They had become acquainted on the train and likely felt a kinship with each other, so if they were allowed to quarantine together, their conversations probably centered on their new surroundings and the men and children they had left behind.

Figure 11.1. The first building Eleanor saw at the Oakdale Reformatory for Women was its administration building. The institution looked more like a country estate than a prison.
HB-0321-E Chicago History Museum, Hedrich-Blessing collection.

PRISON REFORM

Caught up in the circumstances of their own lives, Eleanor and the other inmates were unaware that they had become participants in a progressive social experiment in prison reform. In 1930, at the Oakdale Reformatory's dedication, the Illinois State Superintendent of Prisons clearly stated that the institution would be "a place where women could be sympathetically studied, trained, and disciplined in an effort to restore them to wholesome womanhood." The word "wholesome" was not defined, but, considering the source, it meant law abiding.

A proposal for a state reformatory for Illinois women had been initiated years earlier, in 1916, when several Illinois women's groups lobbied the state legislature for the needed funds. At the time, incarcerated women were held in county jails or the Joliet Prison, where a punitive environment made it impossible for the reformers to bring their social experiments to fruition. The women's groups asked for nearly one million dollars for the reformatory's construction, which the Illinois 55th General Assembly finally granted in 1927. The founders preferred the word "reformatory" over "prison." Their mission was "to return unfortunate girls and women to society—clean, healthful, and with character reconstructed." Little did they know that, in Eleanor's case, their intent would work, but not the way the legal system had planned.

The state funding provided for a five-member advisory board composed of three women and two men. The board members' duties were to assist in selecting a suitable site, to make recommendations as to architecture and furnishings, and to help in the selection of the reformatory's superintendent. Then, upon completion, the members would be required to visit the institution at least twice a year to inspect the grounds, buildings, and equipment, as well as to investigate the treatment and condition of the incarcerated women. After each visit, the board would report to the Illinois Department of Public Welfare.

In 1929, the board facilitated the purchase of farmland near the town of Dwight, then signed off on the hiring of Illinois State Supervising Architect C. Herrick Hammond and his architectural and engineering staff. The team then designed and built the administration, industrial, and service buildings, as well as eight residential "cottages" and a few farm structures. These initial buildings were completed in 1930. Contractors had hired local stone masons, bricklayers, and laborers, giving a welcome boost to the small town's economy.

A reporter for the *Dwight Star and Herald* described the distinctive Normandy-style architecture as follows:

> *The reds, browns, and tans of the masonry were enhanced by the deep brown of the hewn oak timbers used in trimming the entrances, doors, and gates, and by the multi-colored slate roofs laid in uneven fashion to an appearance of age and ruggedness. Chimneys and towers of the same stone set off the sharp gables and complete the castle-like appearance of the structures. The architects were particularly proud of the hand-carved detail of the main entrance of the administration building in oak, colored a deep copper shade by use of creosote stain.*

Each of the "cottages" was named for a prominent woman, including Frances Willard, former president of the Women's Christian Temperance Union; and Clara Barton, Civil War–era nurse and founder of the American Red Cross. Five of the cottages were designated specifically for white women, with three for black women, although none of the inmates' classes, work assignments, or other activities were segregated. Four rooms in one of the cottages were reserved for "unruly women, drug addicts, or those who may develop insanity after being admitted." Each cottage housed fifteen to twenty-eight inmates and also had living quarters for a female "warder." Her duties were the same as a "warden," the more familiar term currently used to describe a staff member in a penal institution.

The entire reformatory property was surrounded by a wire fence that a newspaper reporter noted was "easily climbable" and served merely "to indicate the boundary lines of the reformatory property." Another writer noted that the purpose of the fence was "to keep meddling persons out rather than to restrain the inmates." Two tower houses, in front of the Administration Building, looked, at first glance, as if they sheltered guards, but they were used instead for ornamentation and a place to store garden and lawn tools. There were, however, three unarmed guards—one during the daytime and two at night. Of the staff that numbered more than fifty, the guards were the only men employed on the grounds.

The Oakdale Reformatory for Women had opened on November 24, 1930. Perhaps the most glowing description of the reformatory in its early days was given by a reporter for the *Dwight Star and Herald* who wrote, "An ideal community, where gloom has no place, where the [Great] Depression is an unreality belonging to the outside world, where smiles take the place of harsh words and the inhabitants work, laugh, sing, dance, and play together in almost absolute harmony."

SUPERINTENDENT HELEN H. HAZARD

In searching for a qualified woman superintendent, the members of the reformatory's advisory board determined that their candidate had to possess three qualities—"wisdom, experience, and personality." Thirty-five-year-old Helen H. Hazard was the board's first choice and was appointed by Illinois Governor Louis L. Emmerson in 1930. Even before the reformatory opened, she was on site overseeing its construction.

Superintendent Hazard was an Illinois native; had graduated from Augustana College in Rock Island, Illinois; held a master's degree in psychology from Columbia University, in New York City; and had previously worked in reformatories in Pennsylvania, New York, and Connecticut. She also had worked as assistant superintendent of a federal government reformatory in Alderson, West Virginia. Her extensive education was in sharp contrast to those of the inmates, many of whom had had not passed the fourth or fifth grades. The board members described their new superintendent as "a woman of poise, personal charm, and power; young enough to have retained her enthusiasm, [and] old enough to know *what life has meant* [author's emphasis] to the pathetic womanhood cared for in this reformatory."

How much, though, did the reformatory's first superintendent really know about life? She seemed popular with the inmates, but her own life experiences, compared to theirs, were sheltered and far removed. An article in the *Dwight Star and Herald* recorded an exchange between the newspaper's reporter and the newly appointed superintendent about a "toothless gray-haired woman with a weather-beaten complexion who poisoned her daughter in order to collect on her life insurance money." When asked why the inmate ended up in the reformatory, Superintendent Hazard responded, "Like so many women here, about 150 of them, she is here through the bad influence of some man who got her in his power."

It's possible that Superintendent Hazard thought the same of Eleanor having been under George's influence. That may have, at least partially, been true. But the superintendent had never been a single mother during the Great Depression, nor at any other time. Most likely, she never had a man pay her rent. She may not have had much, if any, experience with men. When the reporter asked about another inmate whom the superintendent had indicated was one of the reformatory's "nicest girls," she commented that even though the "girl" led singing in the "Protestant Group," she was sentenced to the reformatory because she had kept a house of prostitution. "It seems unreal," Superintendent Hazard told the reporter. "I can't understand it."

Perhaps what Superintendent Hazard couldn't understand were relationships between men and women. A similar state of affairs became the story line in a 1955 film titled *Women's Prison*. The plot exposed a philosophical clash between Superintendent Amelia van Zandt (a harsh and unfeeling prison superintendent played by actress Ida Lupino) and Dr. Crane (a caring male physician played by actor Howard Duff). Both Ida Lupino's character and Superintendent Hazard were of similar age, unmarried, and attractive, but there never was any indication that Hazard's work (unlike that of the film character) was anything but exemplary. Still, the excerpt here, regarding a women's prison's fictional superintendent, gives insight into a lack of understanding of human nature that no newspaper reporter would have written about at the time.

Dr. Crane: "May I tell you what's wrong with you? You dislike most of the women here because, deep down, you're jealous of them."

Superintendent van Zandt: *"That's absurd!"*

Dr. Crane: "You're feminine, attractive, and must have had opportunities to marry. Maybe you even cared for someone, once, in your cold way."

Superintendent van Zandt: *"How dare you."*

Dr. Crane: "But, possibly, he turned to someone who could give him what he really wanted—warmth, understanding, love. There's hardly a woman inside these walls who doesn't know what love is."

Superintendent van Zandt: *"Yes, and that's why most of them are here."*

Dr. Crane: "Exactly, even the broken wrecks have known some kind of love. And that's why you hate them."

REFLECTION

Eleanor's two-week quarantine allowed her time to settle in and recover, somewhat, from the stresses of her arrest and trial. In the quiet country setting, it's easy to imagine her reflecting and replaying, in her mind, the past few days of her life. Likely, she thought of George and how pitiful he had been during his sentencing, when he tried to convince the judge that she was not involved and shouldn't be punished. Her role may have been to distract the shop owner, but if George hadn't started carrying a gun, she may not have ended up in Oakdale.

Eleanor had only known George for eight or nine months, and she likely thought back to their good times together, but Richard had been a close friend for years. Although he must have been distraught when he was pressured by the police to tip them off to George and Eleanor's hideout, he continued to be good to her—driving her boys to Hattie's in Sioux City and signing his name on the affidavit for the Change of Venue Petition at her trial. One can picture him trying to lift her spirits by expressing his hope for an appeal or a pardon, as he (likely) saw her off on the train. For the present, though, Eleanor must have felt some relief to have shed her notoriety and just be a number. Even though she and Richard were no longer together, she could think about him. Perhaps, too, he thought of her.

WORK ASSIGNMENT

Superintendent Hazard made a point of meeting every new inmate and learning their names, so she would have visited Eleanor during her quarantine. Joining the superintendent was her assistant, as well as the members of the "classification committee" that also included a parole officer. They evaluated all new inmates for their temperaments and skills, as everyone was required to have a job. Ideally, each inmate would gain experience in a field that would give her the skills to become self-supporting after her release. Unlike Eleanor (who had the longest sentence of any of her fellow inmates), many had been sentenced to only a few years.

The inmates were allowed to state what kind of work they wanted to do, but their choices weren't always granted. Eleanor had years of experience as a waitress, but, at Oakdale, the inmates took turns waiting on each other. With that option off the table, she was told that she would be placed in another line of work. Some women sewed in the shirt factory, where finished products were shipped to other institutions. Others, all skilled seamstresses, were tasked with making every article of clothing worn by the inmates. Some helped with canning food. Women who preferred to work outdoors found themselves tending the twelve-acre garden, harvesting hay in the fields, or caring for the institution's 130 sheep and two thousand chickens.

As Superintendent Hazard told one reporter, "Women love to work in the greenhouse. Many seem to soften under its influence." Whether or not Eleanor chose her job is unknown, but she ended up assigned to the reformatory's laundry.

Eleanor soon learned that the laundry had all the latest equipment, including thirty-two commercial-size electrically powered machines to wash and dry the two tons of sheets, towels, and clothing used weekly by more than 230 inmates. Only ironing was done by hand. All laundry workers wore blue-and-white blouses and bloomers, deemed practical work attire by the reformatory's administration. How things had changed since Eleanor's childhood when bloomers would have been unthinkable, and no one would have imagined that laundry could be washed in machines.

Eleanor may have reflected, too, on the back-breaking work done by her mother, Amelia, when she washed the family's clothes by hand. As a young child, Eleanor had watched her struggle to carry kettles of hot water from the family's wood stove to her washtub, where she'd scrub one item after another from a never-ending pile of work clothes. Perhaps Eleanor also had fleeting memories of sitting on the back steps of the family's home, watching as her mother hung sheets and clothing on the clothesline. The little girl may have run around under the drying clothes, as she played hide and seek with her siblings and simply enjoyed her freedom.

Figure 11.2. These inmate laundry workers obviously enjoyed their work. Dwight Historical Society.

CHAPTER 12

A Room of Her Own

WHEN LET OUT OF QUARANTINE, ELEANOR EITHER WAS MOVED TO ONE of the eight brick-and-stone "cottages" or to the slightly newer and semisecure "cell hall" that had bars on its windows. Newcomers and visitors, alike, were impressed with Oakdale's buildings. A reporter for the Bloomington, Illinois, newspaper (that served central Illinois) wrote, "Entering the grounds one might assume that he was visiting a college campus or a very wealthy residential district of a city." The buildings were designed, as another newspaper reporter explained, "to promote an atmosphere of decent living, a taste for the comforts of home, and a desire to become of service to society as a means of gaining the opportunity to possess a home." At Oakdale, all cells were called "rooms." For the first time in Eleanor's life, she had a room of her own.

RULES AND ROUTINE

Eleanor's room was small, but it had a bed, lamp, rocking chair, rug, closet, and a small table. She was glad that she had a window, and it even had a curtain. Her room faced north and looked out to trees and landscaped grounds. The rooms opened into long corridors that led to stairways, showers, and toilets. None of the rooms had their own toilets or sinks, but inmates were supplied with chamber pots that they were responsible for dumping in the morning. The inmates were required to clean their own rooms, too, and they worked with each other to maintain the common areas.

On her shelf, Eleanor placed her most prized possessions including two photos of herself with LeRoy and LaVerne. She wondered if she ever would see them again but was relieved that they were with Hattie. Next to the photos, Eleanor set her radio and her Amos 'n' Andy box. When she caught a glimpse into other inmates' rooms, she was surprised that the reformatory allowed, as one newspaper reported, "frilly pillows, photographs of movie stars, and potted plants." The number of photographs was limited to six.

The comforts of home, however, were offset by the reformatory's strict routine. Superintendent Helen Hazard and her administration controlled every minute of every day with regulated times for working, eating, and seclusion. Locked in her room that first evening, Eleanor was told that she could have her light on to read, sew, or listen to her radio until 8:30 p.m. Then she had to turn off her light, but she could lie in bed and listen to her radio until 9 p.m. After that, she had to stay in bed (unless she needed to use the chamber pot) until the morning. Cigarette smoking was permitted in the rooms, but nowhere else.

A bell or alarm woke the inmates in the morning. Then, at 7 a.m., a staff member unlocked the inmates' doors. Newspaper reporters didn't mention personal hygiene or bathing, but after the women were dressed for the day, they filed downstairs to the living room of their hall or cottage, where they were allowed to visit with each other for exactly five minutes. The living rooms, in the hall and the cottages, were furnished with sofas, wicker tables and chairs, chandeliers, table lamps, a fireplace, and even a piano with both popular and classical sheet music. When a bell announced breakfast, the inmates entered their buildings' "sunny" dining rooms, where they sat at tables that seated four women. Each place setting included "gay-colored" napkins. The inmates, including Eleanor, took turns waiting on tables, bringing food grown, canned, and often cooked, by inmates.

Six days per week, immediately after breakfast, all the women were off to work or school assignments—four hours in the mornings and four in the afternoons. At noon, the inmates returned, briefly, to their rooms and were locked in and counted, to make sure no one was missing. When the doors opened, they again gathered in the living rooms for exactly five minutes, then went to the dining rooms for dinner, their main meal of the day. Afterward, they resumed their work or returned to school. Supper, at 5:30 p.m., also was preceded by another five minutes of social time.

Whenever possible, Superintendent Hazard required all inmates to learn to read and write. Several of the women were illiterate, so they started with the basics, but first they had to get the staff psychologist's approval based on aptitude and IQ (intelligence quotient) tests. According to the reformatory's records, Eleanor's score was 109, considered high-average. She wasn't required to attend school, but she chose to take classes at the seventh-grade level, as that's as far as she had gone in school as a child. Commercial classes, coordinated with those in the Dwight High School, included typing, stenography, stenciling, and practice in using a Dictaphone. Eleanor's time was split between school and her work in the laundry.

Occasionally, a woman would arrive pregnant at Oakdale. After giving birth in the reformatory's hospital, her baby was cared for by the nurses. The mother was allowed short daily visits, but she still had to fulfill her work assignments. After a year, young children were sent to the inmate's family members or to foster homes.

WHITE STOCKINGS

Superintendent Hazard and her "classification committee" ranked all inmates from "A" to "E," according to their behavior. New arrivals, including Eleanor, started with a "C" classification. The superintendent's policy was to promote inmates to a "B" or an "A" rating within one year, providing they maintained good behavior. According to the reformatory's records, she raised Eleanor from "C" to "B" on December 2, 1933, then to "A" on March 2, 1934. A good record might even result in an inmate being moved to a more desirable room, such as a corner room with two windows. In order that inmates with "A" ratings could easily be recognized, they were required to wear white stockings. All other inmates wore black stockings. A black-stocking woman could not walk on the grounds unescorted unless a woman with white stockings accompanied her.

Some women received money from family and friends or earned a meager amount (three cents per hour) working in the shirt factory. The

Figure 12.1. Superintendent Helen H. Hazard (second from right) posed with three of her inmates. Their uniforms indicate work in the kitchen or other domestic duties. Department of Corrections, "Dwight Correctional Center—Prison Photographs," Record Series 243.301, Illinois State Archives.

inmates' money was deposited into accounts in their names, but they couldn't spend it freely. Those with "A" classifications were allowed to withdraw two dollars per week to spend in the reformatory's commissary, open only on Saturday afternoons. There, they could buy candy, as well as two packages of cigarettes. Class "B" women could only withdraw one dollar of their own money, while class "C" women were allowed fifty cents. Both class "D" and "E" women could spend twenty-five cents. Approximately one-third of the women, possibly Eleanor included, had no money at all.

While good behavior raised the women's ratings, unacceptable behavior resulted in demotions to lower classifications. The main reasons for demotions were "violating smoking rules, extreme impudence or insolence, fist-fighting, attempted escape, or assault." In addition to demotions, women also received demerits. Those were made for "minor

Figure 12.2. Other reformatory inmates were photographed in a corn field. Department of Corrections, "Dwight Correctional Center—Prison Photographs," Record Series 243.301, Illinois State Archives.

impudence or insolence, tardiness, untidiness, or other types of uncooperativeness." Each demerit lengthened a woman's sentence by one day. For the few who had life sentences (or Eleanor with her 199-year term), demerits were used to curtail privileges.

All the nuances of classification boiled down to Superintendent Hazard's philosophy of rewarding good behavior. In a report on Eleanor a few years after she was admitted, the superintendent wrote that her behavior was "excellent." By that time, Eleanor had worn white stockings for some time.

RECREATION

Despite all the rules and regulations, recreation also was important at Oakdale. On Sundays, during the summer, the inmates from the hall and various cottages competed in baseball games. They also could play croquet and pitch horseshoes. In the winter, some inmates even put on theatricals that one of the warders, in an article for the Bloomington newspaper, stated was "safe expression under wise supervision." Some women liked to read and were allowed three books per week from the reformatory's library. Others did "fancy" sewing, including needlework and embroidery. Foreign-born immigrants often brought skills such as lacemaking from the "old country" and were encouraged to teach their crafts to the others.

In addition, there were several alternatives for inmates who didn't want to spend every evening in their rooms. Every other Saturday, they could attend classes in folk, ballroom, and tap dancing. Worship services were provided on Thursday evenings to Catholic, Episcopal, Christian Science, and Lutheran groups, as well as members of Bible classes. On Sundays, Catholic Mass was observed at 7:30 a.m. A Protestant service at 4 p.m. included the inmate choir, as well as spirituals sung by a group of black inmates. Tuesday evenings were set aside for community singing and a discussion of current events. Apparently, all of the evening activities were enthusiastically attended, except for Mondays. That was the night for mending. According to the superintendent, "mending night was not a big success."

OFFENSES

From previous comments that Superintendent Hazard had made to the press, she apparently believed that women naturally were more moral than men. But when one of them strayed, Hazard was quick to suggest that a man had led the woman astray. Of forty or so different types of offenses committed by inmates during Oakdale's early days, the most numerous were murder and manslaughter. A reporter asked Superintendent Hazard about the women who committed these violent crimes, and she said that many of them had killed their husbands. Did the superintendent assume that the women had lovers who turned them against their husbands? Without personal experience with the intensity of intimate relationships, the superintendent would have found it difficult to understand the strong emotions that might have led inmates to murder their husbands even without prompting from another man.

On March 25, 1936, a *Chicago Tribune* reporter wrote a glowing report on conditions at Oakdale. As an example of the effect of prison discipline, he presented the case of Tillie Klimek, then fifty-eight years old, who in 1923 was found "guilty of husband murder and sentenced to life." The reporter stated:

> *This squat little prisoner, who, the evidence showed, had poisoned three husbands and sent a fourth to the hospital, sat in the sunlit swing room of the industrial building yesterday in a dainty-blue-stripped cotton dress. Tillie was making American flags which are supplied to other state institutions. Her smile showed resigned contentment. Judge Marcus Kavanaugh said in sentencing her that she would kill another man. She has a desire to see men with whom she was living suffer, but when she is among women, she is affectionate and popular. His diagnosis has proved correct, according to her record and her popularity among the women.*

After murder, the next largest category of offenses was larceny, which included robbery, burglary, embezzlement, and shoplifting. Added together, the murder, manslaughter, and larceny cases accounted for more than half of the inmates' sentences. Some of the lesser charges included drug violations, prostitution, and vagrancy, with one woman sentenced for starting a fire in a jail. Many of the women, ages sixteen to seventy-five years, were given terms of six months, one year, or from one to fourteen years.

MEANWHILE, IN THE OUTSIDE WORLD

Eleanor wouldn't have been aware that on September 7, 1933, only five days after she arrived at the Oakdale Reformatory, the *Sioux City Journal* published a short article titled "Sioux Cityans to Aid killer: Will Strive to Obtain New Trial for Eleanor Jarman." In its entirety, the article read:

> *An effort to obtain a new trial for Mrs. Eleanor Jarman, "blond tigress," recently convicted in Chicago of murder, is being made by several of her Sioux City friends. She was convicted last week of assisting her sweetheart to kill Gustav Hoeh and sentenced to 199 years in prison. George Finch, an attorney, was said to have left Sioux*

City for Chicago, presumably to take part in the fight to gain a new trial for Mrs. Jarman.

The "friends" who hired the forty-nine-year-old politically ambitious Iowa attorney were unnamed, and Finch's name never appeared in any court documents relating to Eleanor. Perhaps not enough funds were raised to pay his fee, or maybe he thought the effort would be futile.

For other Sioux City news, Hattie was Eleanor's lifeline to the outside world. As her primary correspondent, Hattie may have discreetly included updates from Richard Slater. Reformatory records show that Eleanor also corresponded with her other sister, Frieda, with her brother Otto's wife Dorothy, and with one of Eleanor's sons, likely LeRoy. All were made aware that every incoming and outgoing letter was read and censored by Oakdale's staff.

Inmates could receive whatever letters were sent to them, but they only were permitted to write one letter per week. All correspondence, both ways, had to be written in English. Both incoming and outgoing mail actually was read by two staff members—the official "mail censor" and the warder in the cottage or hall where the inmate lived. These women sat, with scissors in hand, and cut out any references to other women in the reformatory, any severe difficulties in the inmates' families, and any topic that might upset the inmates. Similar censorship applied to visitors. Their conversations had to be audible and spoken in English, as staff members listened to every word.

Eleanor probably was unaware that Chicago's "crime war," and her part in it, still made the news. On October 15, 1933, the *Chicago Tribune* published a two-page spread titled "Chicago Courts Drive Back the Mountain Wave of Crime." The article congratulated the judges on keeping the "wheels of justice humming." The reporter stated that since the beginning of the crime war, on August 1 (four days before Gustav Hoeh's murder), "the criminal court has cut red tape in an amazing manner, imposed prison sentences on 331, and sentenced five killers to the electric chair." The *Tribune* even published a photograph of the Cook County Jail's chair and called it "the end of the road for the killer." Many additional photographs accompanied the story, including one of gangster

Al Capone (then in a federal prison) and another relating to the kidnapping of aviator Charles Lindbergh's baby.

Given equal coverage with these and other high-profile cases was a photo of Eleanor, captioned, yet again, as "the blonde tigress." At the same time, and even with the continued press coverage, new court-appointed attorneys were preparing to appeal her case (as well as George's and Leo's) to the Illinois Supreme Court. At Oakdale, Eleanor simply was called Eleanor and/or number 692. She had begun to adjust to her new routine and probably enjoyed having her own room. Even Superintendent Hazard would have realized that her well-behaved inmate wasn't a vicious killer.

CHAPTER 13

Supreme Court Appeal and George's Execution

FOR GEORGE, THE WHEELS OF JUSTICE, ALTHOUGH NOT ENCOURAGING, were still in motion. While Eleanor adjusted to her new routine at Oakdale Reformatory, George remained in his cell on death row in the Cook County Jail. In the county's early days, death was by hanging, but in 1928, when the new jail opened, Cook County installed a brand-new state-of-the-art electric chair. A reporter described it as "a big-straight-backed-cruel-looking chair, much like an ornamental seat one would expect to find in a millionaire's reception room." With approximately two executions per year, the chair remained in use until 1962, when executions were, instead, carried out by lethal injections.

LEGAL MANEUVERS

George had used the aliases of both "George Kennedy" and "George Anderson" in the hopes of hiding his identity from family and friends. At some point, however, George's father, John Dale, learned of his son's arrest, trial, and death sentence. Perhaps George's sister, Margaret Hull, had kept him informed, as she still lived in Chicago and, no doubt, listened to the radio and read the newspapers. On September 21, 1933, a *Democrat-News* reporter from the Dale family's hometown of Fredericktown, Missouri, wrote, "John Dale, aged father of George Dale who is under sentence to be electrocuted in Chicago next month for the murder of an aged grocer [*sic*], left Monday afternoon for Chicago to see what he can do toward saving the life of his son."

The reporter added that John Dale was "uncertain how to proceed" other than to urge that his son's sentence be commuted to life in prison. He would, however, have a conference with George's latest public defender and with the state's attorney. He also considered having a meeting with Governor Henry Horner in Springfield, Illinois, although it's not known if he did. "Mr. Dale tells us his funds are very low, but he is willing to spend every cent he has on behalf of his boy," added the reporter. "Mr. Dale further states that George has not written him since he got into the trouble, apparently believing that he is keeping his aged father in ignorance of his plight and thereby sparing him the suffering such knowledge would bring."

On September 25, 1933, George's third defense attorney, David A. Riskind, filed a "Petition to Vacate Judgment Against George Dale," asking a judge to set aside both George's judgment and his death sentence and to grant him a new trial. With the attorney's help, George wrote up a petition explaining that he had prepared his defense solely with his first defense attorney, Joseph P. Power, who had left the case after his father died. George also wrote, "Your petitioner further states that he was entitled to a fair and honorable trial and was entitled to be represented by counsel who would have time to fully prepare the defense, more so when the gravity of the offense alleged, and the penalty demanded, was considered." The petition also pointed out that George had been sentenced at the end of the court's August term, not allowing his second defense attorney, Frank J. Ferlic, enough time to prepare an appeal.

Several more legal documents followed. In Attorney Riskind's "Brief and Argument for Plaintiff in Error," he wrote:

> *It is respectfully submitted that the judgment on the verdict should be reversed and a new trial granted for the following reason: that the plaintiff in error did not have that fair and impartial trial to which he was entitled; [and] that the remarks of the State's Attorney were improper appeals to the passion and prejudices of the jury and went*

*far beyond any facts proved in the record and inflamed the minds of
the jurors against the plaintiff in error.*

These and related documents were included in the December 1933 Illinois Supreme Court proceedings titled *The People of the State of Illinois
vs. George Dale, otherwise known as George Kennedy; Eleanor Jarman, and
Leo Minneci—Brief and Argument for Plaintiff in Error.* The judge denied
George's petition, but Attorney Riskind's legal maneuvering had given
George a temporary stay of execution.

ILLINOIS SUPREME COURT APPEAL

In *The People of the State of Illinois vs. George Dale, et. al.*, George's attorneys also hashed and rehashed many points of Eleanor, George, and Leo's
joint trial. Attorney Riskind supplemented his argument with documentation from other cases and argued the following:

- There was no opportunity for George's second defense attorney
  (Frank J. Ferlic) to prepare for trial. "When Attorney Ferlic was
  thus abruptly appointed to take over Dale's defense from Mr.
  Powers," stated Attorney Riskind, "he should have demanded a
  continuance in order to have time in which to become prepared
  and in which to acquaint himself with the client's story."

- The court allowed the admittance of "incompetent, irrelevant,
  immaterial, and highly prejudicial evidence." Attorney Riskind
  stated that the ballistics expert had connected the crime with a
  pistol from which one bullet was fired, "but no bullet was found
  in Gustav Hoeh's body, so there was no proof that the bullet from
  the pistol was the fatal bullet." Attorney Riskind continued, "The
  other three guns should not have been entered into evidence, as
  they had no connection to the crime. . . . It is altogether possible
  that the bullet which passed through Hoeh's body has never been
  found." [Actually, the coroner's inquest revealed that two bullets
  had passed through his body.]

- Police officers made arrests and seized weapons without search warrants. Attorney Riskind contended that the officer who testified did not have reasonable grounds for his belief that Eleanor and George were guilty of the murder.

- The other robberies were not admissible in evidence. Attorney Riskind noted, "The parade of eleven witnesses was calculated to affect the minds of the jury against the defendants and was highly improper trial practice, as well as prejudicial to Dale."

- Appeals made to the passions and prejudices of the jury are grounds for a new trial. These improper comments from the prosecuting attorney included his asking the jury to help along a so-called "campaign" against crime, regardless of the actual guilt or innocence of the defendant or defendants.

All these points, and others, were rebutted (with documentation from other court cases) by Illinois Attorney General Otto Kerner. After Attorney Riskind's defense, the attorney general concluded, "The evidence shows a cold-blooded murder committed pursuant to a robbery, and we respectfully submit that the judgment of the court below should be affirmed." The outcome didn't affect Eleanor, at Oakdale Reformatory, or Leo, at Joliet Prison. George was taken back to his cell in the Cook County Jail, not knowing, at the time, how long he would have to live. Back in his hometown, the Fredericktown reporter wrote, "The people of this community are saddened over the fate that has overtaken George Dale," adding that nearly everyone in the town knew him.

On February 23, 1934, the Illinois Supreme Court set the date of George's execution for April 20, 1934. Meanwhile, three inmates of the Cook County Jail cut a hole with a hacksaw in a steel wall. Their attempt to escape was, according to jail officials, known to nine other men, including George. No names of the other men were given, but a newspaper writer jumped on the story and reported that, because of the attempt, George was locked in solitary confinement. While he had nothing to do but look at the four walls of his cell, the gardens at the Oakdale Reformatory began to reveal a few crocuses and other early spring flowers. And, in Garfield Park, where George had memories of walking with Eleanor and her sons, the fruit trees would soon be in bloom. The beginning of spring signaled the renewal of life, but George wouldn't be alive to see it.

Preparation for Execution

George had five living siblings, but only his sister Margaret, with whom he had lived at the time of the 1930 federal census, was in Chicago. There was no mention in the newspapers as to whether she had attended her brother's trial, nor is it known if she visited with him or wrote to him in jail. But on April 11, 1934, Margaret appeared before the Illinois Board of Pardons and Parole, in Springfield, Illinois, after George's father had circulated a petition among his son's friends in Fredericktown. Represented by an attorney, George's family and friends asked that his death sentence be commuted to life in prison.

Their pleas, however, fell on deaf ears. An *Associated Press* article titled "Governor Horner Refuses Clemency to George Dale: Slayer of Chicago Merchant to be Electrocuted April 20" was published in newspapers all over the country on April 14, 1934. A reporter wrote, "Mr. Horner today declined to intervene in the case and refused Dale's plea for a commutation to a life sentence."

Two days earlier, on April 12, 1934, Judge Philip J. Finnegan had ordered the Warden of the Cook County Jail to permit Doctor Harry R. Hoffman, director of the Behavior Clinic of the Criminal Court of Cook County, "to examine the above-named defendant, now confined in the County Jail, as to his mental condition and make his report to the Court on or before April 19, 1934." The reason for the examination was "Question of sanity." Dr. Hoffman's report of the psychological examination of George Dale, prisoner number 916, was completed on April 17, 1934. Although signed and approved by Dr. Hoffman, the exam was performed by his assistant, Dr. Harry A. Paskind and filed by the Criminal Court of Cook County under CR 70149.

The results of the psychological exam are as follows:

This patient is examined in the death cell of the Cook County jail.
He is found sitting at a table reading and writing, apparently quite

calm, and when called to the examination he says at first that he does not want to bother with an examination because he is not going to make any plea of insanity, that he is perfectly sane, but when told the examination will not do any harm, comes to the examination willingly. During the examination he is quiet, calm, co-operative, polite, answers questions promptly and relevantly, and gives information regarding himself as follows.

His name is George Dale, born in Mississippi [should be Missouri], June 28, 1905 [date not verified, but likely 1903]. His father is living at 74, not in good health but patient does not know the details; the mother died at 50. He has 3 sisters and 2 brothers, all in good health. As far as he knows there have been no persons in his family in an institution for the insane, feebleminded, or epileptic, and none of them was alcoholic.

He says he started school at 7, left at 22 or 23 and finished 2 years of high school. He never failed to pass, was an average student. By trade he has been a radio assembler; the longest he ever held one job was 7 years, and he worked last at his trade in 1932, and has done odd jobs since. He says he is single. he knows of no previous illness except measles—denies gonorrhea or chancre [syphilis]. He denies the use of alcohol, tobacco, or drugs.

He says he was arrested only once and that was on a charge of murder. He was tried before a jury, found guilty and sentenced to the electric chair, and that he is to go to the electric chair on the 20th of April.

He says he sleeps well, eats well, is not worried nor frightened. He makes no complaints referable to nervous or mental disease and questioning elicits none. He gives the place and time correctly as the County Jail, Tuesday April 17, 1934. He gives 3x3 is 9, 4x4 is 16, 5x5 is 25, 6x6 is 36, 7x7 is 49, 8x8 is 64, 9x9 is 81, 10x10 is 100, 12x12 is 144. He names the president as Roosevelt, the governor as Horner, the mayor as Kelly, the largest city as New York, and the largest river as the Mississippi. He names the oceans as the Atlantic, Pacific, Indian, Arctic, and Antarctic.

DIAGNOSIS—No mental disease—not committable as insane or feebleminded.

DAY BEFORE EXECUTION

George's execution was one of three scheduled for shortly after 5:00 a.m., on April 20, 1934. First would be twenty-one-year-old John Scheck, the bank robber who, during a court hearing (in July 1933) for another crime, tried to escape and in the process shot and killed a police officer. According to the *Chicago Tribune*, that officer's murder was what had prompted the court's "war on crime." During John Scheck's last day, he was visited by sixteen relatives. In a letter to all of them, he wrote, "Please smile and laugh, for that's all that you now can do. If you'll be happy, I'll be happy, too. I have only myself to blame." But in another letter, addressed to the general public, he blamed his downfall on the economic depression and excused himself because he was "only a boy."

As the *Tribune* reported, George, who would be next, spent the previous evening writing a short letter to Eleanor, stating, in part, "I wish to thank you for all the happy moments we have spent together." Then he sent his love to her and to the two boys. Because Superintendent Hazard, at the Oakdale Reformatory, had instructed her censors to cut out any mention of "severe difficulties in the inmates' families and any topic that might upset the inmate," it's questionable as to whether Eleanor ever received his letter. Another *Tribune* reporter, in 1951, wrote that on the evening of George's execution, all radios (at least in Eleanor's building) in the inmates' rooms had to be turned off so that Eleanor would be spared hearing about George on the evening news.

George also was given the unusual task of filling out much of his own death certificate. All death certificates have a place for the name of the "Informant," and in that space George wrote "himself." He gave correct information for the names and places of the births of his parents, and he correctly stated his previous occupation as "radio worker" at "Stewart Warner." He stated that he was "male, white, and single," and his previous address was "4300 W. Madison." But he continued to be vague about his date of birth. For the month and day, he wrote "Unk," for unknown, and, this time, for the year he wrote "1906." Someone else later filled in his cause of death—"Electric shock, legal execution."

Of the three men on death row, jail officials noted that George was the only one to joke and laugh, and that he "appeared the most buoyant." He told an Iowa reporter that he had turned to robbery because he was bored with factory work. Perhaps he was saving face as it was more likely that he had lost his job during the Great Depression. Both George and the third man, thirty-five-year-old Joseph Francis (who murdered a milk wagon driver during a robbery), boasted that they would "go to the chair like men." John Scheck, the youngest of the three and the first to be executed, was "the least composed."

Joseph, the milk wagon driver murderer, wrote to the jail's warden and thanked him for his kindness. From midnight to 5 a.m., the men were confined in their "death cells," only a few feet from the execution room. One reporter looked in at George and noted, "Dale lay morosely on a cot listening to dance music from a small radio." During the night, each of the three men met with religious leaders. George, like Eleanor, was Lutheran. The other two men were Catholic. The reporter added, "After these talks, the killers were treated to a special dinner. Scheck did not eat."

EXECUTION AND AFTERWARD
Reporters in attendance wrote that the execution of all three men was completed in half an hour. One reporter, from Farmer City in central Illinois, got a front-row seat and noted that 150 people were crowded into a "tiny place" behind a heavy sheet of glass. Also in attendance were Norman and Earl Hoeh, the sons of Gustav Hoeh. Before each execution began, a priest chanted, "May God have mercy on your soul." Then, in the words of the Farmer City reporter, came the first execution:

> John Scheck, a ruthless killer at 21, was slowly marched into the room, a deputy on either side. He was dressed only in trousers and underwear—his pant-legs were cut off—he was slapped into the chair, strapped tightly—a steel cap fit over his head which was shaved—a dark mask hid the features of his face.

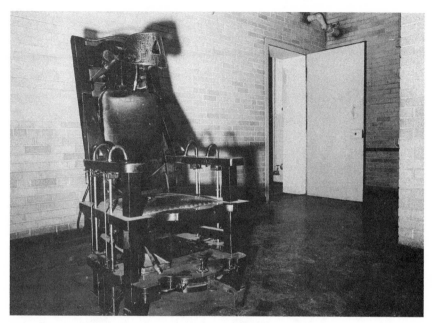

Figure 13.1. The electric chair at the Cook County Jail was used for executions from 1929 until 1962. ST-13001416–0008, Chicago Sun-Times collection, Chicago History Museum.

The assistants stepped back—the sheriff snapped his fingers— everything was clocklike—a clanging sound, like the closing of a steel door, broke the terrible silence. Scheck, who killed and robbed, bolted in his strappings—his fists clinched the arm of the chair in an iron grip—29,000 volts of electricity were going through his body—the first "shock" lasted 40 seconds—it seemed 40 centuries to me—there was a moment of rest and then 9,000 more volts were sent through the man's body—another rest—9,000 more volts—five physicians examined the body and finally pronounced him dead. His limp form was dragged from the chair, and he was carted away to the county morgue where the members of his family finally claimed his body.

The reporter spared his readers the details of George's execution, only to say, "The procedure was the same—terrible, horrifying, he, too, was carried away." George, simply prisoner number 916, took six minutes to die and was pronounced dead at 5:18 a.m. During the execution of the third inmate, a man in the "audience" fainted. The reporter concluded by stating, "If all wrong-doers, hoodlums, gangsters, and some of the more frivolous among our youth could see a real execution, much of today's crime would be blotted out."

That evening, George's body was the only one still in the morgue, as the families of the other two had taken them for burial. Three days later, George's sister Margaret claimed his body. After a short funeral, she had him buried in Chicago. The *Chicago Tribune* stated that he was taken to Oak Lawn Cemetery, but his death certificate reads "Oakwoods Cemetery." Neither cemetery, however, has a marker for him nor any record of his interment. Wherever he is, in the words of the priest, "May God have mercy" on his soul. Outlaws Bonnie and Clyde were gunned down in their Ford on May 23, 1934, slightly more than a month later.

CHAPTER 14

Eleanor Requests a Pardon

BY THE SUMMER OF 1934, FRESH GREEN GRASS HAD GROWN OVER George's recently dug grave. Dandelions briefly showed their yellow colors, but, almost as quickly, they morphed into a sea of fluffy white seeds. Oak and maple leaves of red, yellow, and brown covered the ground in the fall. While some of the leaves blew away, others matted and stuck together before they were blanketed with snow. The changing of the seasons had covered George's remains, and his gravesite blended in with other unmarked graves. Perhaps George's sister, who knew the location, came to visit and to remember.

Eleanor also remembered George, but there's no way of knowing if she thought of him fondly or if she was bitter that, as Superintendent Helen Hazard believed, most women with murder sentences had acted under "the bad influence of some man." Indeed, the *Los Angeles Times* had recently published a well-illustrated two-page spread by female writer, Frances M. Kelly, titled "Life Fades Fast for Gangsters' Molls." Eleanor, described both as the "blonde tigress" and the "sweetheart of George Dale," was pictured alongside Bonnie Parker (partner of Clyde Barrow) and Evelyn Frechette—"part-Indian sweetheart of John Dillinger." The *Times* story began, "Just as there's fire where there's smoke, there's invariably a moll where there's a gunman! So, in crime, too. It's always 'cherchez la femme!'" The French phrase translates to "search for the woman," implying that to track down a gangster one first needs to find his female companion.

A Model Prisoner

Meanwhile, life went on as usual in the Oakdale Reformatory. In the spring of 1935, inmates working on "the farm" provided the institution's kitchens with garden-to-table produce including crisp radishes, tender peas, and fresh lettuce. Others tended to hundreds of baby chicks. In the summer, the women gathered eggs and harvested loads of fresh corn and juicy ripe tomatoes.

For part of the day, Eleanor kept up with her classes in the institution's school, while she also continued her work in the laundry where she was one of fifteen workers. The reformatory's in-house newsletter, the *Trail Blazer*, boasted of the laundry's latest equipment that included washing machines for both 150-pound and 300-pound loads. White sheets and clothing even got a final rinse of bluing before being extracted and dried. The work for Eleanor and her fellow inmates was unending.

The women's days, however, were not all school and work. In the summers, they gathered on screened-in porches for buffet suppers, and each residence cottage or hall held their own "wiener" and marshmallow roasts. Throughout the year, the staff prepared and decorated birthday cakes for each woman. Eleanor's birthday was on April 22, and, in 1935, she turned thirty-four years old. Years would pass, though, before reformatory records correctly reflected her 1901 birth date due to her vague remarks in court and on various documents as to where and when she was born.

Every four months, the reformatory's classification committee reviewed each of the inmates. In the *Trail Blazer*, Superintendent Hazard's secretary gave the committee her highest praise. "An endeavor is made," she stated, "to give each woman some insight into her difficulty, and assignments to classes are made on the basis of the recommendations which the professional group makes to the administrative group." The superintendent continued, "One of the many advantages which it [the committee] affords is the opportunity each woman has to appear before the committee at which time she is permitted to discuss fully matters pertaining to her schedule, other aspects of her life here, and her plans for the future."

PARDON REQUEST

In the spring of 1935, Eleanor and the classification committee's parole officer discussed the possibility of Eleanor requesting a pardon from the governor of Illinois. There was no reason for her not to apply. The committee continued to give Eleanor an "A" rating, and its members stated that she "had gotten along unusually well." Superintendent Hazard likely surprised a *Chicago Tribune* reporter (who was used to the "blonde tigress" description) when she told him that Eleanor was "one of the most tractable inmates," meaning that she was both docile and obedient.

Parole Officer Martin M. Keegan officially wrote Eleanor's *Petition for Commutation of Sentence* on June 21, 1935. Then he filed it on her behalf. The two-page application for executive clemency was addressed, "To His Excellency, Henry Horner Governor, State of Illinois," and it was date stamped "received" the following day. After briefly restating the facts of the case, Officer Keegan, writing for Eleanor, stated:

> *I was jointly indicted with Leo Minneci, now serving time at the Illinois State Penitentiary, Joliet, Illinois, and George Dale who was electrocuted, charged with the murder of Mr. Gustave [sic] Hoeh. I feel that my case was not properly presented to the court by the Attorney who was appointed for me, and together with the antagonistic attitude of the newspapers, I did not receive a fair trial. The newspapers stopped at nothing to blacken my name.*
>
> *The facts in this case are: On the morning of August fourth, in company with the aforementioned Leo Minneci and George Dale, I stopped at the deceased's place of business located at 5948 West Division Street, Chicago, with the intention of purchasing some shirts. I was in the act of examining these shirts when I heard the fatal shot fired. I was not aware that these two men contemplated a hold-up of this store when I went in there with them. Sometime prior to this, these men had warned me if I ever divulged their original activities, they would murder me [author's emphasis], and on this particular morning in question they intimidated me to the extent that I was forced to ride in the automobile so as to ward off suspicion that they*

might contemplate robbing a place. However, at this particular store it was their intention to purchase shirts.

The salient fact I wish to present for your consideration is that I had no knowledge these men contemplated robbing the deceased, Mr. Hoeh, and, in reality, I was only a bystander. I have served since September 1933 and pray that your Excellency may see fit to commute my sentence. I have presented briefly and clearly all facts pertinent to this case and pray your Excellency to be merciful.

Eleanor's personal appearance before the Illinois Division of Pardons and Paroles was on July 9, 1935. If her travel to the hearing, in Springfield, Illinois, was handled like that of another inmate who left the reformatory to testify in a court case (and was written up by a local newspaper reporter), Eleanor was accompanied by her parole officer, as well as a male guard. They either drove or took a train for the 124-mile trip. Eleanor certainly would have enjoyed the change of scenery. Likely, they stayed overnight, and Eleanor (as had the other inmate) spent the night in a holding cell in the Sangamon County Jail, while the prison officials stayed in a hotel. For Eleanor's appearance at the hearing, she wore one of the print dresses made by her fellow inmates.

Eleanor's petition was her first, and only, official statement saying that she had been intimidated by George and Leo. And it is the first, and only, time she said they had threatened to kill her. She also contradicted her earlier testimony by stating that she planned to purchase shirts when, previously, she said she was only looking at neckties for her boys. Apparently, her parole officer didn't read, or pay attention to, her former testimony. The document was witnessed by staff member and future parole officer Margaret Schlosser, as well as two other women from the Oakdale Reformatory.

INPUT FROM THE PUBLIC

Anyone from the public who wanted to attend the hearing was welcome. The only person who showed up, though, was Earl Hoeh, one of the sons of the victim, Gustav Hoeh. Earl Hoeh's short and to-the-point testimony before the Pardons and Paroles board was as follows:

Mr. Hoeh: I received notice Eleanor Jarman was petitioning. I don't know for a pardon or for what in particular, but on behalf of my mother and my brother and myself, I come down to ask you to refuse any clemency. My dad was 71 years old.

Mr. Dickman: Was he one of your relatives?

Mr. Hoeh: My father.

The Chairman: This is in connection with George Dale?

Mr. Hoeh: Yes sir.

Mr. Dickman: You are here in protest?

Mr. Hoeh: Yes sir.

Mr. Dickman: All right. She came down in 1933 and got a 99 [*sic*] year sentence.

Mr. Hoeh: Yes sir, and I would like to take back to my mother the fact it will be denied.

The Chairman: That is something we will have to determine later. We will advise you later.

Mr. Hoeh: Thank you very much, gentlemen.

Earl Hoeh was the only person to speak against Eleanor's request for commutation, and there were no letters against setting her free. Instead, six character witnesses wrote letters in favor of her petition. One letter was from a former coworker, and one from her boys' former doctor (who also had been a friend of the victim, Gustav Hoeh), while the four others were from members of Richard Slater's family. Eleanor's former boyfriend was proving to be a very good current friend, as well. Obviously he had not forgotten her, as it appears that he rounded up his family to come to her aid. All of the letters of support were written to Mr. W. C. Jones, chairman of the Division of Pardons and Paroles, Springfield, Illinois, and all the letter writers lived in Chicago.

Mrs. Elsie Burrus, 2850 Walnut Street (former coworker) wrote:

I'm writing in behalf of Mrs. Eleanor Jarman of Dwight Reformatory. I understand a parole is being considered. I have known Mrs.

Jarman for ten years and knew her to be a hard worker, a trusted employ [sic], and a kind mother to her two children. I worked with her for two years, and she was faithful and honest. She has asked me to see other friends in her behalf, but my husband is seriously ill in Hines's Veteran Hospital, so I am helpless to do much for her, altho I know she deserves another chance more than anyone else I know. Won't you please give her case special consideration?

Another letter was sent from Elmer K. Avery, M.D., 3165 West Madison Street, Eleanor's boys' doctor. He, like Superintendent Hazard, believed that her actions were "due to the influence of her associate." The doctor wrote:

For about one and one-half years before this woman's conviction, I saw her quite often where she worked and, on several occasions, treated or examined her two boys. She was always well-liked and steady at her work and always did the best she was able to keep her boys in school and well-dressed and always insisted that they be man-nerly and well-behaved. I never saw anything vicious or criminal in her behavior, and whatever she may have done I believe was due to the influence of her associate.

From what I knew of her and her work and care for her boys, I believe the public would have nothing to regret if she was given her liberty, and I feel confident that she would return to the care of her boys. For myself, I wish to say that the man, Mr. Hoeh, that her asso-ciate killed, was a patient and good friend of mine for years. I have been a practicing physician in Chicago for 35 years and express my opinion of Mrs. Jarman out [of] the experience I have had in judging people. Thanking you in advance.

Then came the letters from Richard's family. There was no way of know-ing, at the time, how important this man would become in Eleanor's future. Richard's connections with gamblers likely kept him in the back-ground, but his family's letters, written in 1935, proclaimed four-, five-, and six-year friendships with Eleanor dating back to 1929. First was

Mrs. Goldschmidt (Richard's sister, Hermina), at 1415 North California Avenue.

Hermina Goldschmidt agreed with the praise already given by Eleanor's coworker and by Dr. Avery. She wrote:

> *I am writing in reference to what I know about the character of Eleanor Jarman. My husband, family, and I have known her approximately five or six years. To our knowledge, she always was a good mother to her children and always worked. She met the wrong kind of people, as up until about four months before that (her trouble), I had seen her almost daily after she had lost her last job. And she was always [an] honest and trustworthy person. Hoping that this will help her get her freedom.*

Hermina's letter begs the question of what Eleanor was doing after her last waitress job and before her crime spree with George and Leo. What circumstances had brought Eleanor together with Hermina and even with Hermina's husband and family? Did Richard take her to visit his relatives for family meals and get-togethers? Were they all involved in Richard's window display business where Eleanor had answered his phone? The answers to these questions and others remain unknown.

Another letter was from Darrell Goldschmidt (stepson of Richard's sister Hermina), at 3215 Warner Avenue, who wrote:

> *I have known Elenore [sic] Jarman who comes before your board for parole Tuesday 9th. I have known Elenore [sic] for six years, and I can truthfully say that practically all the time I have known her, she had been working as a waitress. I never would have realized that she would become entangled in such an offense because she was an ideal mother to her two children and always seemed to put them before everything else.*

Mrs. Lula Herzfield (wife of Richard's brother Max/Mack Herzfield), at 4923 Sheridan Road, wrote:

I hear the case of Elenore [sic] Jarman is coming before your board soon and wish to say that I have known her for about six years. She was always an honest hard-working woman and did her best to raise her two boys as they should be raised. I know that she had been out of work for some time when she got into this trouble, and I think that she was just misled. I am quite sure it will never happen again if she gets her freedom, and I can't believe half of the things that were said about her at the trial as I knew her well and never knew her to be cruel in any way.

Then there was this letter from Mrs. Ollie Cox (mother of Lula Herzfield), at 4921 Sheridan Road, who wrote:

In regard to Mrs. Elenore [sic] Jarman, I have known her for about four or five years and never knew her to do anything wrong and always seemed to be fond of her two sons and good to them and worked and tried to support them and herself best she could. I couldn't say anything against her, and if she could ever be free again, I feel that she could be trusted.

MERCY NOT DESERVED

After Eleanor's hearing, the *Chicago Tribune* picked up an *Associated Press* story from Springfield, Illinois, titled "Eleanor Jarman Pleads Commutation of Sentence." It read, "Eleanor Jarman, the 'blonde tigress,' serving a term in Dwight reformatory for a Chicago holdup murder, today sent to the state pardon board a petition for commutation of sentence. Earl Hoeh, son of the man slain in the robbery, appeared before the board to declare that mercy is not deserved."

With her parole officer and the guard, Eleanor returned to Oakdale Reformatory where she waited, uneasily, through the rest of July, then August, and then September. Finally, on October 23, 1935, more than four months after her hearing, the Division of Pardons and Paroles issued the following statement: "Subject: Eleanor Jarman, 692-Dwight. Please be advised the Governor has this day denied the application for executive clemency filed to the July 1935 term of the Pardon Board in the case of the above named."

Earl Hoeh's brief testimony against clemency had carried more weight than Eleanor's six letters of support. But Eleanor wasn't alone in being denied her request. The day after the governor's announcement, an *Associated Press* story picked up by newspapers all over the country stated that Eleanor was one of four women and one of eighty-two "murderers" from the state of Illinois who were denied clemency. One of the other women was Vera Carl, who had ridden with Eleanor on the train from Chicago to Dwight immediately after her sentencing. Vera had been sentenced to fourteen years for plotting her husband's murder. Even with the denial, though, she would be out in twelve years, while Eleanor's 199-year sentence still meant life behind bars.

Hopefully, Eleanor's parole officer showed her the letters written on her behalf. If so, Eleanor would have taken comfort in knowing that Richard's family supported her in her appeal for freedom. And, in her heart, Eleanor would have known that Richard, himself, was behind their efforts, as well.

CHAPTER 15

Margaret, a Fellow Felon

ON THANKSGIVING DAY, 1937, SUPERINTENDENT HELEN HAZARD invited her inmates to watch a movie. From then on, movie nights were held weekly at the Oakdale Reformatory. In 1939, a list of films shown to date was published in the reformatory's annual *Trailblazer* newsletter. First was *Ramona*, a romantic comedy from the end of the silent film era, followed by *Maytime*, a 1937 musical drama. None of the films had dark themes or anything to do with crime. By the fall of 1939, Oakdale's inmates had watched nearly one hundred films. Then they were treated to a brand new release—the now-classic musical fantasy *The Wizard of Oz*.

In the beginning of the film, actress Judy Garland's character, Dorothy, clutched her dog Toto and imagined an escape from her family's midwestern farm. In its opening scene, filmed in a drab monochrome, Dorothy broke into the now well-known song "Somewhere Over the Rainbow." Suddenly, a tornado lifted the farmhouse, with Dorothy and Toto inside, then dropped it, and them, in an unknown land. Audiences were thrilled when scenes burst into vivid color, and the girl and her dog found themselves in a fantasy land. At that point, Dorothy told Toto the obvious—that they "weren't in Kansas anymore."

There is nothing to suggest that any future decisions made by the reformatory's inmates were influenced by *The Wizard of Oz* or any other film. However, by viewing bits and pieces of life on the "outside," Eleanor and the others could vicariously enjoy the freedoms expressed by the film's characters. By September 1939, Eleanor had served six years in the reformatory and had watched the release of several women who had

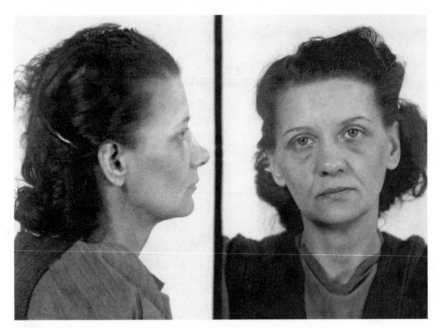

Figure 15.1. Margaret Keringer was admitted to Oakdale Reformatory under her alias of "Mary Foster." Parole and Pardon Board, "Institutional Jackets," Record Series 403.002, Illinois State Archives.

become her friends. For some, their dreams had come true, but Eleanor was still doing the laundry.

"Mary Foster" and Her Many Aliases

Oakdale's revolving door swung the opposite way, as well, with a constant stream of new inmates. One, who arrived in January 1939, was "Mary Foster," although she had twenty or more names and aliases that ranged from her maiden name of Margaret Keringer to her married name of Margaret Makaron (also spelled Mackeron), to others she made up including "Freda Nerson," "Vicky Kellman," and "Annie Dubeljonski." When she was admitted to the reformatory as number 1409, she recently had been sentenced to one to ten years for the latest of her many crimes—shoplifting a purse from Marshall Field's Department Store in Chicago. She was placed in Eleanor's cell hall, a few doors away from Eleanor's room.

Margaret was a couple of years younger than Eleanor and one of ten children, all born in Hungary. Both women were slender and petite. Other than coming from a large family and being separated, but not divorced, from their husbands, she and Eleanor had nothing in common. Margaret's shoplifting offense was minor compared to her previous crimes. She had been incarcerated in other states for grand larceny, including bank robbery. She was a hardened criminal and had twice escaped from authorities. She also seemed an unlikely friend for Eleanor, still considered by the administrators a model inmate. Perhaps, because their rooms were near each other's, the two women became acquainted in the five-minute social time before meals. Margaret may have sought out Eleanor because of her previous notoriety as the "blonde tigress."

A report from the Federal Bureau of Investigation that was inserted into Margaret's "prison jacket" from Oakland Reformatory stated that "her husband is reputed to have started her out on a career of crime, and her specialty is taking employment as a domestic and then stealing furs, jewelry, and anything of value from wealthy families." At Oakdale, the classification committee assigned Margaret to work in the fields. She also sewed in the shirt factory and attended school.

If Margaret had divulged her background, Eleanor would have learned that in December 1921, then seventeen-year-old "Margit" Keringer was one of 476 passengers packed into the steerage deck of a large luxury liner, the S.S. *Orbita*. After entering New York harbor, the British ship docked on Pier 42 on Manhattan's lower west side. In America, the teenager would use the name Margaret, and the only person she knew, at the time of her arrival, was her sister Julia, who had preceded her to New York City.

Then, in May 1924, and supposedly after a brief flirtation, Margaret married Polish immigrant Jack Makaron/Mackeron in New York's City Hall. Her marriage to the naturalized American gave her American citizenship. The couple married again, six months later, in a Catholic Church in Dayton, Ohio. In between thefts and burglaries, she and Jack had five children, including their first, who died the day after she was born.

The 1930 federal census showed the couple living in the Bronx, New York, with the three children who were part of the family at that time. In

August 1931, four months after the birth of her fourth surviving child, Margaret was arrested for grand larceny—stealing from her employer while working as a maid. Jack supposedly helped her choose residents who owned valuables. Ironically, he had described himself to a 1930 federal census taker as a "self-employed clothing dealer."

At Margaret's subsequent trial, Jack made the newspapers because he "created tumult in the courtroom" when he lunged at the judge on the bench. One newspaper reporter called him a "bull-like sort of fellow." Margaret was sentenced to two and one-half to five years at the Auburn State Prison for Women, in New York. She served part of her term, as well, at the Bedford Hills Correctional Facility. Jack was unable to provide for the children, so they all became wards of the City of New York before being placed in a Catholic home for dependent children.

Margaret was released in August 1933, the same month that Eleanor, George, and Leo were arrested and put on trial in Chicago. But as soon as she got out of prison, she was rearrested on a previous grand larceny charge and brought back to court. The judge offered to free her if she agreed to the terms of her parole and if her husband could provide her with a home. At first, Margaret said she'd go the Salvation Army, but then she reluctantly agreed to go with Jack, and they left the courtroom together. They separated soon afterward, and neither claimed the children. Jack disappeared, and Margaret moved into the Stinson Hotel, in Detroit, Michigan, with a man named Walter Allen.

A LENGTHENING RAP SHEET

In May 1936, in violation of her parole and now calling herself Margaret Allen, she and five so-called gang members robbed the Detroit Savings Bank. The Detroit Police arrested Margaret and put her in the Wayne County Jail for casing out the bank prior to the robbery, as well as hiding some of the stolen money after the heist. During this same time, police were investigating her previous reported thefts in Detroit and elsewhere. She had continued to hire out as a domestic and steal from her employers, and she was charged with larcenies totaling approximately $5,000. Margaret's victims were residents of Detroit and Highland Park,

Figure 15.2. Margaret posed for this photo sometime during the 1930s. Courtesy of Michael S. Makaron.

Michigan; South Bend, Indiana; Jersey City and Hoboken, New Jersey; and New York City.

Unlike thefts of valuables, Margaret's bank robbery charge was a federal offense, as the bank's funds had been federally insured. In July 1936, the US Marshals Office stepped in and took Margaret into custody, with the intent of transporting her to a federal facility. A narrative of her "rap" (record of arrest and prosecution) sheet in the Oakdale Reformatory records states, "On October 20, 1936, the deputy United States Marshal from Detroit reported that he had *lost* [author's emphasis] Margaret Allen while en route to the Federal Institution for Women at Alderson, West Virginia."

When the details appeared in a syndicated newspaper article, readers learned that Margaret had escaped from a train. A reporter wrote, "When the train stopped at Charlestown, Virginia, the woman [Margaret] asked to go to the rest room, Chief Deputy Marshal John B. Grogan said. His wife, he said, accompanied her, and as soon as the door was closed, Miss [Margaret] Allen leaped through the train window and fled." Within a few months, a Delaware County, Pennsylvania, newspaper reported on a possible sighting, adding that the escapee was five feet two inches tall and weighed 104 pounds. The article referenced a wanted poster stating that Margaret's "underworld nickname" was "dumb Maggie."

Ten months after Margaret's escape from the train she turned herself in to the FBI, apparently unable to cope with being a fugitive. The agency then sent her to the Federal Detention Farm in Milan, Michigan, southwest of Detroit. According to the *Detroit Free Press*, in addition to her already pending charges she faced an extra five-year term under the Federal Escape Act. While at the detention farm, she became what prison officials called "a trouble-maker."

During an "outbreak" in October 1937, Margaret (still Margaret Allen) and a woman named Ruby Allen (no known relation) threw hot coffee and dishes at two other women. Margaret's rap sheet continued:

There has been, since the arrival of Margaret Allen, considerable unrest among the women due in part because of the superiority complex of [the two other women] Mae Scheible and Nelle Muench.

Margaret Allen is a dangerous woman, has had previous prison experience and is facing a term for escape from the Marshal and is wanted in several states.

It was necessary to send male officers to look after her and lock her in her cell, and the officers were cussed out proper. She ripped blankets and finally divested herself of all clothing. The bed was taken from her cell, as well as everything of any danger to herself. Both Margaret Allen and Nancy Hanks have threatened to kill Nelle Muench and Mae Scheible, either here or when they get out.

On February 1, 1938, authorities transferred Margaret Allen to the Cincinnati Workhouse where she escaped again. A report from the Oakdale Reformatory, after she was admitted under the alias of "Mary Foster," continued:

On May 30, 1938, it was found Mary ["Margaret Allen"] had escaped during the previous night, having forced a hasp in the women's quarters and reached the laundry where she procured a ladder. She scaled a wall and escaped. A guard making regular rounds of inspection passed her bed several times without suspecting anything was wrong. Next morning a dummy made of bed clothes was found in it.

When Margaret was arrested yet again, in December 1938, after shoplifting in the Marshall Field's store, a *Chicago Tribune* headline read "Seize Housemaid As a Shoplifter, Find Bank Bandit." An accompanying article confirmed that the "mild-looking woman" used at least twenty aliases, and that her stolen loot, while working as a domestic, totaled nearly $30,000. Although Margaret's shoplifting charge was enough to incarcerate her, the "stolen loot" included a mink coat, a jade ring, a diamond ring, and numerous other items of clothing and jewelry from several Chicago-area victims.

Prior to Margaret's trial, several of the Chicago victims identified her, in person, at the Detective Bureau of the Chicago Police Department—just as Eleanor, Leo, and George's robbery victims had identified them on the "show-up platform" at the Austin Police station. One of the victims, whose letter is on file in Oakdale Reformatory's records, wrote, "When I talked to the defendant, she asked me what name she gave me, and I told her Annie Dubeljonski, and she grinned. Then she said she never saw me before." Margaret pleaded guilty at her trial in the Criminal Court of Cook County, Illinois, then, as was Eleanor, was sentenced to the Oakdale Reformatory.

MARGARET'S REQUEST FOR PAROLE

Margaret's intake form from the reformatory stated that she had "red-brown" hair, weighed 114 pounds, was five feet two inches tall, and had grey eyes. She spoke Slavic and Hungarian but, as noted, "She doesn't do very well with English." Margaret had a fourth-grade education, had no work history, smoked, and her "disposition" was described as "good and bad." In the space after "associates," a clerk had written "bad." One of them, a former gang member from her bank robbery days, was John Carl Conley. At the time of Margaret's admittance to Oakdale, Conley had been incarcerated for bank robbery as inmate 368 at the US Penitentiary at Alcatraz Island, California.

In January 1940, a year after Margaret arrived at Oakdale, she requested parole. Superintendent Hazard and her committee read her long rap sheet and took into consideration their "knowledge of her personality," then wrote that, if paroled, Margaret's chances of adjustment in community life would be "poor." Even so, as Eleanor had done five years earlier with her plea for a pardon, Margaret faced the parole board.

Instead of letters of support as Eleanor had received, the only letters for Margaret came from her victims, demanding that she remain behind bars. One was from a Chicago woman, an employee in a dental office, who explained that during the time that Margaret had been employed to clean her house, she had jimmied a cedar chest and then opened a tin box that contained a lifetime of the victim's savings. The savings included bonds set aside for the Chicago woman's daughter's education. Meanwhile, the woman had health problems and had to borrow money to pay for a major operation. Still, she traveled to the Michigan prison farm to identify Margaret in a line-up. The woman's letter concluded by stating:

Yet, with all the expense, grief, and aggravation this woman has caused me, I say, in all honesty, that I am not being vindictive in protesting her parole. She has been proven an habitual thief and is therefore a menace to society in general and to housewives in particular. I urge you, therefore, not to give this woman an opportunity to rob and steal from honest citizens. She certainly should be made to serve more than the one year she has served to date.

Even Margaret's own answers to the board's questions didn't help her cause. When she was questioned, she didn't even try, as Eleanor had, to explain her past actions. Instead she said she knew she wouldn't get a break and added, "My record alone hangs me, so it's no use speaking for myself." Yet she did speak, and the following is an excerpt from her transcript:

Question: After you came to this country, what did you do by the way of work?

Answer: Well, I wasn't doing anything at the time.

Question: Did you ever do any work in this country?

Answer: Yes, sir.

Question: When was the first work you ever did?

Answer: I don't remember.

Question: The particular offense for which you are serving is theft of a purse from Marshall Field and Company's store?

Answer: Yes, sir.

Question: How long were you engaged in shoplifting?

Answer: This was my first time.

Margaret's public defender was none other than Frank J. Ferlic, the same defense attorney who had represented Eleanor's "sweetheart," George Dale, after George's first defense attorney had to leave his, Eleanor, and Leo's joint trial. But Attorney Ferlic was of no help, as the State's Attorney also referred to Margaret as a "habitual" criminal and stated that he, too, was opposed to her parole. Even Margaret's parole officer stated that

Margaret was "not expecting freedom by parole but is hoping that some plan may be effected whereby she may be released to the Federal authorities to complete the serving of her sentence at the Cincinnati Workhouse and to return to New York State to answer the parole warrant there. It is not believed she is entirely sincere in the statements she makes regarding her several difficulties."

MARGARET'S SKILLS

At the end of Margaret's hearing, she told the judge, "I would much rather they let me out and not be on parole—not be watched all the time on parole." When a board member asked, "You don't want to be watched?" Margaret replied, "No, I would much rather be free." Then she explained that she'd rather finish out her term than get out early and be on parole. Not verbalized at the time was a third alternative—escape. No one will ever know when she first mentioned the possibility to Eleanor. Did attorney Ferlic tell Margaret that the "blonde tigress" also was at Oakdale?

Margaret's years of crime had taught her some skills. As noted earlier, one of Margaret's theft victims stated that Margaret had "jimmied [forced open with a crowbar] a cedar chest and opened a tin box" in order to steal the family's savings. Then, when she escaped from the workhouse in Cincinnati, she was said to have "forced a hasp"—the hinged metal strap that fits over a staple on a door lock and is secured by a pin or a padlock. Slim and petite, like Eleanor, she also had managed to crawl out of a train window.

Because Margaret's work in the fields took her to the outlying areas of the reformatory, she also knew of the institution's boundaries and, likely, had looked beyond to the woods and corn fields—somewhere over the rainbow—on the other side of the fenced-in property. Other inmates may have had thoughts of escaping from Oakdale, but Margaret had the skills to actually do it.

PART IV

MOST DANGEROUS WOMAN ALIVE

CHAPTER 16

August 1940

ON AUGUST 8, 1940, NATIONAL NEWSPAPER COLUMNIST ED LAHEY AND his wife were driving to their home in Chicago from Carrollton, Illinois, where Ed had covered a story. The Laheys already had driven two hundred miles when they neared the town of Dwight, at 3:30 a.m. Ed was exhausted, so his wife took the wheel, and Ed climbed into the back seat and fell asleep. Suddenly, state police stopped the Laheys at a roadblock. "A flashlight beam shone in my face," wrote Ed in a later column, "and the barrel of a 12-gauge shotgun was an inch from my nose." A deputy explained that two women had escaped from Oakdale Reformatory, and one of the women was Eleanor Jarman.

In 1933, Ed had been one of the reporters who accompanied Eleanor and the three other female inmates on the train from Chicago to Dwight. Years later, in a column, he wrote about meeting Eleanor and said he felt "real compassion" toward her when he said goodbye. But, by 1940, he had put her out of his mind. At the roadblock, when he heard the news of her escape, he noted that he "started to say, hurrah," but then he decided it would be better if he didn't. He never saw her again.

Eleanor had nothing to lose. She'd served seven years of her 199-year sentence. What would Superintendent Helen Hazard and her staff do if she was caught? They could put her back in the reformatory with a demerit or two, but they couldn't increase her sentence.

THE FIRST FEW DAYS

When the superintendent was questioned, she was puzzled as to whether Eleanor Jarman and Margaret Keringer (aka Mary Foster) had planned their escape ahead of time, but it seems likely. In a newspaper article titled "Hunt for 'Blonde Tigress' Turns Toward Joliet Area," a reporter in the nearby town of Streator wrote, "Although she [Margaret] was never known to associate with the 'Blonde Tigress,' prison officials said she had sought of late to be quartered near Mrs. Jarman. Each time her request was denied." To put their suspected escape plan into action, they had to wait for an opportune time. Eleanor's main work assignment was in the laundry, and Margaret worked in the fields, so what could have brought them together on the morning of August 8 when they both were cleaning the staff's quarters? Perhaps they volunteered for the job.

While staff member Etta Tranbarger was inattentive, Margaret, the experienced lock picker, had no trouble getting Eleanor and herself through a normally locked door. In Superintendent Hazard's words, Eleanor was the "tractable" one—a follower, not a leader. The day after the women's escape, the *Associated Press* quoted Hazard emphasizing that Eleanor had been "an industrious, obedient, and model woman in almost every respect." But Eleanor, like Margaret, must have yearned for freedom as well.

Once Margaret and Eleanor got through the door, they stole clothing from the staff's quarters. Then, being careful not to be seen, they left the building they had been cleaning and managed to reach and climb over the reformatory's barbed-wire-topped twelve-foot fence. When they got to the other side, they changed out of their work attire and put on the street clothes they had carried with them. Before the public even knew the women were missing, they had hitchhiked at least to Joliet, having been picked up by unsuspecting drivers along the way. When Ed Lahey and his wife were stopped at the roadblock, Eleanor and Margaret were far, far away.

Reformatory staff learned that Eleanor and Margaret were missing during the institution's mid-day headcount. Staff members were sent outside to look for them, but they quickly realized that the women were not on the premises. The big question in the minds of Superintendent

Hazard and her staff, as well as local and state police and others who heard the news on their radios, was where did the women go to meet their immediate needs? With one of them wearing the polka-dotted dress, and the other the blue suit, they were easily recognizable. As soon as possible, they must have discarded their well-publicized clothing and found something else to wear. They also needed food and shelter.

If Eleanor and Margaret had followed the example of Robert Elliott Burns, the Georgia chain gang fugitive, they may have stolen clothing off a clothesline of a rural farmhouse. They also could have broken into an unoccupied house to find food and perhaps cash stashed away in a cookie jar. Then they could have hidden out for a night or two in an outbuilding or a corn field. If that was the case, they weren't seen, as there was no mention in any news reports of break-ins or sightings.

SUPPOSITIONS

On August 10, Superintendent Hazard told a *Chicago Tribune* reporter of a possible motive for Eleanor—that she had recently learned of the disappearance of her "18-year-old son." The press, however, confused the boys, writing that LaVerne was the oldest, when LeRoy was the one who was eighteen. It's entirely possible, as the superintendent had told the *Tribune*, that "the news [of one or the other of her sons] may have prompted the escape." A matron from the reformatory immediately was dispatched to visit Eleanor's relatives, while police in Sioux City, Iowa, were "on the lookout."

An article on August 11, 1940, in the *Sioux City Journal* alerted residents that the "Blond Tigress May Hide Here." A newspaper reporter from Streator, Illinois, agreed with the supposition and quoted "reformatory authorities" who told him that they, too, thought that "Mrs. Jarman would separate from the other woman and head for Iowa." With the intense police scrutiny, though, it seems unlikely that Eleanor, without a support network in place, would immediately and alone undertake a one-way journey that spanned nearly five hundred miles. And if she had reached her family and if they hid her for a day or two, where would she have gone from there?

A few days later, the *Journal* reported that the Sioux City Police were "puzzled" when they found a "mystery woman" asleep in an automobile in a used car lot. The woman identified herself as Carol Howard from St. Louis, but the authorities said she "partly resembled the escaped convict." They arrested her because, as a reporter stated, "She would not answer their questions and on the theory that she might be the 'Blonde Tigress.'" The mystery woman still wouldn't talk, even after a day in jail while the Federal Bureau of Investigation compared her fingerprints with Eleanor's. After the prints were determined not to be a match, and after the FBI confirmed that the woman had no previous record, the Sioux City police had no choice but to let her go.

Had Eleanor, in the previous seven years, seen anyone in her immediate Sioux City family? Her reformatory records state that she had no visitors at all in her years behind bars, although the distance between her families' homes and the reformatory may have been beyond their means to travel. Whether she wanted to see her family or not was irrelevant, as she was smart enough not to get them involved in aiding and abetting a fugitive. She would have known that instead of risking her own capture and bringing disgrace to her boys, they needed to move on with their lives.

Suppositions about Eleanor's and Margaret's whereabouts quickly made front-page news. A Streator, Illinois, newspaper reporter, who tried to obtain all of the latest details, gave the story a new twist. In his August 9, 1933, article, "Hunt for 'Blonde Tigress' Turns Toward Joliet Area," he wrote, "The 'Tiger Woman' weighs 99 pounds and has yellow bobbed hair and blue eyes. Her weight has varied to a large degree since she was first received at the institution, at one time reaching 144 pounds. Impaired health is blamed for the decline, officials of the institution said, and it is their belief that she will be unable to withstand privation or exposure over any period of time during her new-found freedom."

The Streeter reporter also had been permitted to enter Eleanor's "deserted cell" after her escape and noted that she had left behind "a decrepit radio and two snapshots of the fugitive and her two boys, pictures taken, perhaps, before she drifted outside the pale of the law." An *Associated Press* reporter added that the Oakdale officials no longer thought Eleanor was headed to Sioux City, but instead believed she and Margaret "might be hiding in Chicago."

ELEANOR'S AND MARGARET'S FAMILIES

In preparation for the reformatory's matron to question Eleanor's relatives, Superintendent Hazard and her staff first would have looked up the contact information they already had in their files. Seven years earlier, when Eleanor was admitted, she had given the name and address of her oldest sister, Mrs. Joe (Hattie) Stocker, as next of kin. At the time, Eleanor's sons, LeRoy and LaVerne, were in Hattie's care. The reformatory also had on file the name and address of Eleanor's other sister, Mrs. Ray (Frieda) Baker, but the files only listed names, not addresses, of Eleanor's five surviving brothers. Eleanor's parents were deceased, and all of her siblings except Frieda lived in Sioux City, Iowa.

Without digital information at their fingertips as we have today in the Internet age, the reformatory staff likely telephoned the Sioux City Police Department and asked their assistance in tracking down the addresses and telephone numbers (for those who had telephones) of the various family members. In addition, the Illinois State Police Department likely communicated with the Sioux City Police by teletype, a machine used by law enforcement agencies at the time to send and receive typed messages over dedicated telephone lines.

Today, the addresses of Eleanor's family members in August 1940 are easily reconstructed from the 1940 federal census. Although the census is now transacted by mail, census takers in 1940 physically visited every individual household in the entire country, taking a headcount of the United States's population based on each person's location on April 1. Taken every ten years but only made public seventy-two years later, the census records provide a snapshot in time and are invaluable to today's researchers. The 1940 census was made public in 2012, and Eleanor and her family, in April 1940 (four months before her escape), show up as follows:

- Henry Berendt, forty-nine years old and Eleanor's oldest surviving brother, was a lodger in the home of Anna Ford, an unemployed divorcee. Henry, also divorced, worked as a butcher in a meat-packing plant. He had no children.

- Hattie Berendt Stocker, age forty-seven, was the wife of Joseph Stocker, a "head driver" in a meat-packing plant. Living with them was their twenty-three-year-old daughter Bertha. The Stockers' sons, George and Joseph Jr., had moved out of their parents' home, but also lived in Sioux City. Both worked in meat-packing plants, and both were married. Daughter Gertrude Stoker Day, also married, had moved to Omaha, Nebraska, where she lived with her husband, a conductor on a street railway.

- Otto Berendt, age forty-five, was a butcher in a meat-packing plant. He lived with his wife Dorothy and stepdaughter Dorothy Seifert. Eleanor's son LeRoy Jarman also was listed as part of Otto's household, but that year's census records showed the eighteen-year-old boy *"temporarily absent."* LeRoy had been discharged from the Civilian Conservation Corps six days prior to April 1, and his whereabouts in the interim were unknown.

- Alfred Berendt, age forty-three (twin of Frieda), lived with his sister Hattie and was a "scale man" at the stockyards. He had no children.

- Frieda Berendt Baker, age forty-three (twin of Alfred), lived with her husband Raymond Baker, their son Lionel, and their daughter Shirley in Minneapolis, Minnesota. Raymond was a window washer for an office building.

- Frank Berendt, age forty-one, as did several others in the family, worked in a meat-packing plant. He was one of five lodgers in the home of J. J. McRaynold, a livestock buyer. He had no children.

- John Berendt, age thirty-three, was divorced, had no children, was a cook in a restaurant, and lived in the New Howard Hotel.

Eleanor also was listed in the 1940 census. On April 1, she was one of 282 "inmates" (along with forty-eight staff members) at the "State

Reformatory for Women," in Dwight, Illinois. This was just before her thirty-ninth birthday, but her age was incorrectly given as thirty-six.

The staff at the Oakdale Reformatory attempted to revise the contact information for Eleanor's sons, but they didn't get all of it correct. Although LeRoy and LaVerne lived with Hattie after Eleanor was sent to the reformatory, neither of the boys stayed with their relatives the whole time. At some point, LeRoy had been admitted to the Iowa Training School for Boys, in Eldora, Iowa, 176 miles due east of Sioux City. The mission of the juvenile detention facility (now the Boys State Training School) was to "reform wayward youth through hard work and educational opportunities." Reformatory records state that he was "paroled sometime in 1939 to his aunt." The aunt either was Hattie or her brother Otto's wife Dorothy, as LeRoy shows up as a member of Otto's household in the 1940 census.

LeRoy's eighteenth birthday was on September 24, 1939. Ten days later, on October 4 (either before or after he completed his parole; records are unclear), he began his six-month term in the Civilian Conservation Corps (CCC) at a work camp in Whiting, Iowa, thirty miles southeast of Sioux City. According to his CCC records obtained from the National Archives, the reason he gave for joining the Corps was "to have a job; to have a home." He left blank the line that asked for the occupation of his father but, poignantly, wrote that his mother was a "housewife."

The Corps provided LeRoy's bed, board, and medical care. In addition, he and his fellow workers each were paid $30 per month, but the government agency only allowed them to keep eight dollars of their monthly earnings. If LeRoy was like some of the others who later were interviewed, he spent his eight dollars on candy and snacks. LeRoy's remaining $22, in the form of monthly allotment checks, were sent to his uncle Otto, listed in his CCC records as next of kin. LeRoy's file shows a satisfactory work record in soil conservation, as well as an honorable discharge, even though he left one week earlier than his scheduled term. The reason, as stated, was "for convenience of [the] government." Perhaps the CCC ran out of work for him to do. LeRoy's last day in the Corps was on March 25, 1940.

Adding insight to Eleanor's motivation to flee was the *Sioux City Journal* article "Blond Tigress May Hide Here" that speculated that, after her escape, she wanted to see her son "*LaVerne*" [author's emphasis] "after learning that he had been discharged from working in the Civilian Conservation Corps." As previously stated, however, LeRoy was the son who had served in the CCC. As of April 1, 1940, the census listed LaVerne a "ward" of Sarah Mayhew, a seventy-five-year-old widow who managed a farm near Sioux City. She must have taken over as his guardian after the boy ran away from Hattie's home and then was returned (as noted in yet another newspaper article) by a sheriff. After reading reformatory records and newspaper reports, one has to wonder how often clerks and reporters confused LaVerne with his brother.

Eleanor had only one other family member, and that was her husband, Michael Roy Jarman. Eleanor's census data (that may or may not have been correct) stated that she still was legally married in 1940, even though she and Michael Roy had been separated for fifteen or more years. In prior court testimony, Eleanor had said that she didn't know, and didn't care, where he was. She may not have known at the time of her arrest that he and "Edna," listed in the 1930 federal census as Michael Roy's wife, also were living in Chicago. But shortly afterward, the couple moved to the Mississippi River town of Muscadine, on Iowa's eastern border. There, in 1940, Michael Roy worked as a laborer on a Works Progress Administration storm sewer project. Although there is no known record of his divorce (or remarriage), he claimed in the 1950 federal census (released in 2022) that he had married Edna in 1934 and that they had three sons.

Margaret, who had proven herself to be good at escaping, was not savvy enough to live for long "on the lam"—running from the police. After her previous escapes, she either was recaptured, or she found that being a fugitive was so unbearable that she had no choice but to turn herself in. If she had encouraged Eleanor to escape with her because of Eleanor's notoriety, Margaret was, however, smart enough to know that staying together was too risky. One can imagine them hiding out the first night, but then they would have parted ways.

The press didn't mention Margaret's family. With her many aliases, neither the police nor the press may have known that her brother, John

Keringer, was a chef in the Triangle Restaurant at 225 North Wabash, in downtown Chicago. John and his wife Victoria lived on Chicago's south side in a small brick house at 10058 South Vernon Street, at its intersection with East 101st Street. Did Margaret manage to get to her brother's house or, perhaps, to the back door of the Triangle Restaurant where she could have asked for the chef and received a free meal? It's possible. Margaret's only other known sibling was Julia, who lived near New York City. Like Eleanor, Margaret had no idea where her husband was, nor is there any record of them getting divorced.

HOMES OF ACQUAINTANCES WATCHED

Three days after Eleanor and Margaret's escape, the *Associated Press* wrote, "Homes of acquaintances of both women in Chicago were being watched on the chance the two might be in hiding in the metropolis." In one of those homes was another Margaret—Margaret Dale Hull, the sister of George Dale and the family member who claimed his body and saw that he got a decent burial. She lived on the corner of South Marquette Avenue and East 78th Street, on Chicago's south side. Whether the police thought of her as an acquaintance or whether Eleanor even thought of going to her home is not known. The same can be said of women Eleanor had befriended while working as a waitress. She had several acquaintances in the city, but she had never lived entirely on her own or on the street. She needed more than an acquaintance. She needed a real friend.

Harboring a fugitive was, and still is, a crime. When today's investigators look for a suspect in a crime, they look for a person with means, motive, and opportunity. The same was true in 1940, and the person who helped Eleanor after her escape had to have possessed all three of these attributes. In the author's opinion, and after careful consideration of everyone in Eleanor's life, there was only one person who fit. And that was Richard Slater.

After Eleanor's escape, an Oakdale Reformatory staff member revised Eleanor's file to update her personal history. Richard (as "Dick Slater") was listed as "a very close friend." But who would have given reformatory officials that information? Perhaps it was Hattie. As a family member, she would have been questioned by the police, and Richard's name may have come out in the conversation. No other friends were listed. At the time, Richard lived on the second floor of an apartment building at 4660 Broadway, in Chicago, in what now is called the Uptown Square District, with his wife and eleven-year-old stepdaughter.

According to Eleanor's reformatory records, the Chicago Police contacted Richard on October 8, 1940, two months after Eleanor's escape. His address and telephone number were listed in the 1940 Chicago telephone directory, so if he had been at home earlier he wouldn't have been hard to find. Regardless of his location, however, he would have heard of Eleanor's escape like everyone else—by reading the newspapers or listening to the radio. If, however, the two of them had ever discussed the possibility of an escape, perhaps they had an agreed-upon place to meet. In all likelihood, during the two months between Eleanor's escape and the date Richard was finally contacted by police, he was out of the city, providing her with a place to lie low.

CHAPTER 17

Means, Motive, and Opportunity

BEFORE APPLYING THE MEANS, MOTIVE, AND OPPORTUNITY TEST TO Richard Slater, one needs to dig a bit into his past. But which past? Richard was a multifaceted man who walked a fine line between the law and the underworld. He held various jobs that included house painter, taxi driver, woodworker, and store window display decorator, while, on the shadier side, he was known for the poker games he held in his home. He also worked for and kept connections with gamblers and gangsters. While he appeared to have known a lot of people, he kept a low profile. Above all, his family members remember him as a kind and generous man.

Adding another layer of mystique to Richard Slater were his two names. He was born "Nathan Herzfeld" (sometimes spelled Herzfield) to Hungarian immigrants, in Chicago, on December 19, 1900. Nathan wasn't listed in the 1900 federal census, as his birth came eight months after the census was taken, but the census did list his parents Jacob and Minnie, his brothers Max (sometimes spelled Mack) and Armin, as well as sisters Regina and Hermina. His sister Rose was born in 1903. Armin died in his teens, in 1909.

Sometime during or after 1917 and before the federal 1930 census, Nathan Herzfeld changed his name to Richard Slater. Whether the name change was related to serving in World War I, renouncing his Jewish heritage, or dabbling in the underworld is not known, but it didn't interfere with his relationships with his family. Nathan (as Richard) remained in contact with most, if not all, of his siblings throughout the rest of his life.

RICHARD AS ELEANOR'S FRIEND

Without mentioning Richard's first name, Eleanor brought up her friend's last name (Slater) in her August 1933 court testimony. As cited in chapter 9, she answered the question as to how she earned money for rent by stating, in part, "The name of the gentleman for whom I answered telephones is Slater. He is more or less a pretty good friend of mine." She then added, "I do not like to bring an innocent party into this. His business is window displays."

Eleanor also stated in court that she answered Slater's phone at 28 South St. Louis Avenue. The location was just around the corner from the apartment she shared with her boys at the time of the federal 1930 census. According to the same census, Richard Slater's residence as of April 1, 1930, was at 208 North Hamlin Avenue, less than a ten-minute walk from the Paradise Cafe, where Eleanor worked as a waitress from January 1931 until November 1932. Eleanor and Richard both lived and worked in the area of Garfield Park on Chicago's west side.

On the first day of Eleanor and her codefendants' trial, Richard had been one of two signers of affidavits submitted with the Petition for Change of Venue from Cook County. To researchers today, this document offers proof that the man born as Nathan Herzfeld actually was Richard Slater. Years after signing the petition, Richard signed a Selective Service card using the identical signature and added the notation, "alias Nathan Herzfield." See figure 17.1 for a composite image showing the two signatures. They also match Richard's signatures on deeds to property that he would later purchase in Lake County, Illinois.

In addition, the Selective Service card further validates Richard's relationship with the Herzfeld/Herzfield family. In the space in which he was asked for the "Name and address of person who will always know your address," he filled in the name and address of his sister, Hermina (then "Mrs. Goldschmidt"), at 1415 North California Avenue, Chicago. Genealogical research has verified that Hermina Goldschmidt is the married name of Hermina Herzfeld.

Proof that Hermina and others in Richard's family knew, and were fond of, Eleanor is shown in chapter 14, "Eleanor Requests a Pardon." Not only Hermina, but also her stepson, Darrell Goldschmidt, as well

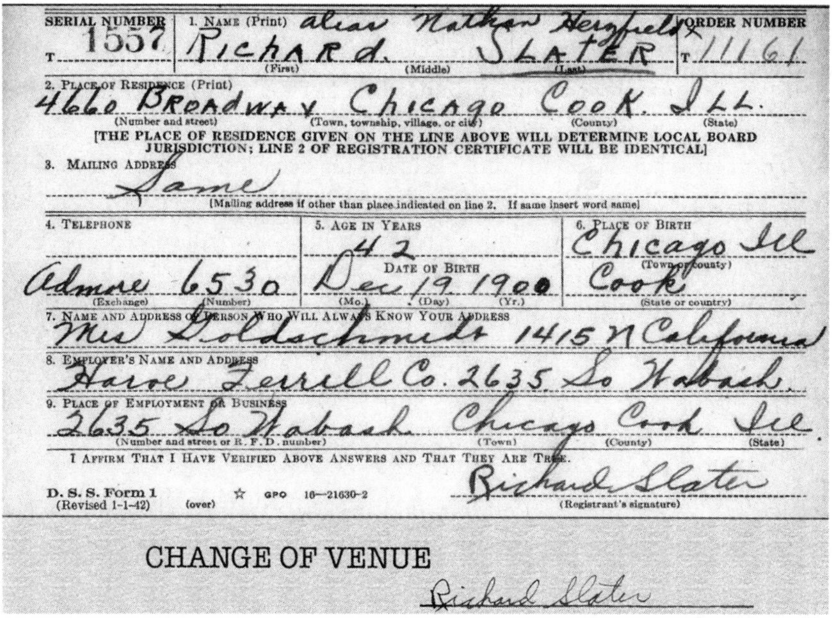

Figure 17.1. This illustration combines Richard Slater's Selective Service card (from 1942) with an image of his signature on the Petition for Change of Venue from 1933. The signatures are the same. Courtesy National Archives at St. Louis; St. Louis, Missouri; WWII Draft Registration Cards for Illinois, 10/16/1940–03/31/1947, Record Group: Records of the Selective Service System, 147; as well as the Circuit Court of Cook County, Illinois.

as Richard's sister-in-law Lula Herzfield (wife of his brother Max) and even Ollie Cox (Lula's mother) wrote letters of support. The extended Herzfeld/Herzfield family defended Eleanor almost as if she was one of their own. The combination of data on Richard's census, court, military, and property records—including his signatures and the family correspondence—all document that the "Slater" mentioned by Eleanor in her court testimony as her "friend" was Richard Slater, alias Nathan Herzfeld/Herzfield.

As stated in chapter 4, a lengthy article in the *Chicago Tribune* on December 15, 1935 (more than two years after Gustav Hoeh's murder), updated readers on Eleanor's part in the crime. Without mentioning Richard Slater's name, the newspaper reporter explained that a tip from

Leo Minneci led to another man who, when questioned, said that he knew Eleanor's former boyfriend, Richard. The other man tipped off the detectives who were waiting in Richard's apartment when he came home from taking Eleanor's boys to Iowa.

Not only had Eleanor and Richard, on occasion, lived and worked together, but Eleanor had been embraced by Richard's family. She had trusted him with her sons, then, after what likely was an intense interrogation, he was forced to give police the information that led to her arrest. Regardless of ups and downs (including Eleanor's fling with George) of their relationship, Eleanor's updated reformatory file was correct. Richard had been, and still was, her "very close friend."

RICHARD HAD "MEANS"

Richard was well connected and financially secure. Unlike many city dwellers who didn't own a car, Richard's drive to Sioux City with Eleanor's boys indicated that he also had dependable transportation. Self-employed and with a variety of skills, he was able to earn a legitimate income without being locked into a time schedule. At the same time, he made money, a lot of money, from illegal gambling. Whether Richard's interest in gambling started under the name of Nathan Herzfeld/Herzfield and/or if it had something to do with his name change is not known. But he had the means to help and hide Eleanor.

As revealed in chapter 10, the news of Richard's participation in gangland activities broke in the *Chicago Tribune* after the murder of gang leader Jack Zuta. According to a *Tribune* article on August 25, 1930, allies of crime boss Al Capone shot and killed Zuta at a Wisconsin hideout on August 1, 1930. Zuta had been Capone's accountant in the mid-1920s, but he later joined forces with gang war rival George "Bugs" Moran, as well as the Aiello brothers, Joe and Dominic.

Zuta, however, had retained his accounting skills, and he kept detailed records of the gambling and bootlegging enterprises, as well as brothels, under his control. After his murder, a judge issued a search warrant and discovered two safe deposit boxes listed under Zuta's assumed name. On August 16, 1930, a *Chicago Tribune* reporter wrote of their discoveries, stating that the boxes were stuffed with documents, canceled checks, promissory notes, books, and gold pieces. Police had found the boxes in basement vaults, in two different buildings, including the gang's headquarters at the American Bond and Mortgage Company on North Dearborn Street.

"Here is presented, for what is believed the first time in the history of gangdom, a concise balance sheet of the operations of a so-called 'mob,'" stated the *Tribune*'s reporter. Payoffs were recorded for several Chicago judges, a judge's attorney, a police sergeant, and a former state senator. Zuta's receipts for one week, all itemized, totaled $429,046.78, more than $7.5 million today. The reporter added, "The first four names on the record—Skelley, Slater, Hale, and Klaproth—were believed to be the names of collectors for the gang." A subsequent article included the men's first names—"Tom Skelly, Dick Slater, Slim Hale, and Charles Klaproth."

Dick's (Richard's) job as a collector required him to visit Zuta's regular customers and pick up gambling receipts, including money from slot machines. Richard's route took him to "resorts in certain sections of the country towns." In the 1930 federal census, Richard claimed to be a house painter, while Eleanor testified that his business was "window displays." These and other occupations may have been legitimate, or they could have been fronts for better-paying gang-related activities.

RICHARD HAD "MOTIVE"

In addition to having the "means," or resources, to help Eleanor and advocating for her at her trial, Richard appeared to be the well-dressed gentleman who saw her off at the train station. It's easy to imagine him telling Eleanor that he would never again give up her location. Two years later, members of his family supported Eleanor with their letters recommending a pardon. Undoubtedly, Richard still cared very much for Eleanor. Perhaps he still was in love with her. If so, his motive to hide and help her after her escape is obvious.

Richard's role in aiding and abetting Eleanor may not, however, have been as apparent to the police. As noted in chapter 16, Richard had married in the interim. The police may have assumed that his marriage indicated that he had moved on from having Eleanor as part of his life.

What the authorities didn't know, though, was that Richard's complex lifestyle allowed room for both women.

Richard had married Beaulah Nell Thompson, a divorcée with two grown children and a seven-year-old daughter, Joy, in 1936. By that time, Eleanor had been an inmate at Oakdale Reformatory for three years and had been denied a pardon. Photographs of Richard and Beaulah show them as a happy couple, but stories have trickled down through the family indicating that Richard hadn't always been faithful. Whether or not he and Eleanor again became romantically involved will never be known, but the pieces of their puzzling lives, when laid out in a timeline, fall into place. It would be difficult to imagine Richard ignoring the opportunity to aid Eleanor when she needed him.

Figure 17.2. Richard Slater was photographed in 1941 on a park bench with his wife, Beaulah. Compare Richard with the man on the train platform in figure 10.2 (in chapter 10). Courtesy Sandra Oliver.

RICHARD HAD "OPPORTUNITY"

"Opportunity" is the third trait in the means, motive, and opportunity test. In hiding and protecting a fugitive—in this case, Eleanor—Richard's advantage lay with his underworld connections and his flexibility to be away from home for various lengths of time. His job as a "collector" appears to have started in the 1920s. It involved visits to Morton Grove and other "country towns" north of Chicago (in both Cook and Lake counties) where he traveled to collect the proceeds from gambling partners.

Not surprisingly, records from the Lake County Clerk's Office show that, in 1946, Richard and Beaulah owned property near Diamond Lake, less than a half-hour's drive due west from the town of Lake Forest. Their property included a still standing small house that had been built in 1920. Whether the small house and outbuildings photographed in 1939 and shown in figure 17.3 are on that same parcel of land is not known, but Richard and Beaulah may have visited or rented the property before they

Figure 17.3. Richard and Beaulah Slater were photographed in 1939 in a rural setting, likely their Lake County retreat. Courtesy Sandra Oliver.

bought it. Richard wore hunting clothes and held a rifle. He definitely was not in an urban setting.

Richard, at least, would have known that a quiet rural area would make an ideal getaway for Eleanor to stay for a few months, or more, until the initial onslaught of media dropped her from its front pages. By then, she would be ready to take on a new identity. After all, Richard had changed his own name, so he was in a good position to help Eleanor do the same.

ON TO CHICAGO

Newspaper reports after Eleanor and Margaret's escape had stated that unsuspecting motorists picked up the hitchhiking women and took them as far as Joliet, Illinois. In 1940, Joliet, thirty miles southwest of Chicago, had a population of approximately forty-two thousand residents, and the surrounding area was still rural. If Eleanor and Margaret had spent the night in an outbuilding or a cornfield, they likely continued the next morning to Chicago where they could blend into the crowds. The escapees knew that police would be patrolling train and bus stations, so they had no choice but to continue to hitchhike, a common practice even for women at the time. US Route 66, now considered a historic highway, passed through Joliet, and then extended into the center of Chicago.

In Eleanor's parole application, Superintendent Helen Hazard noted that Eleanor was "a person without funds," but there's no way of knowing if she had five or ten dollars to her name and, if so, if she took it with her. Margaret, though, was the experienced escapee, and she may have had some money that she shared with Eleanor. Or, if either of the women had told any of the other inmates of their plans to escape as Robert Elliott Burns had done in the film *I Am a Fugitive from a Chain Gang*, one or more of the inmates may have slipped a dollar or two into their hands.

Even without money, though, Eleanor and Margaret could have used the public telephones located in practically every bus station, hotel lobby, and drug store in the country. Behind the doors of the telephones' wooden booths, they would have had the privacy to pick up the receivers and ask for long-distance operators, providing they used false names. If the women reached their parties, they would have had to speak discreetly, as the switchboard operators may have been tipped off to their escapes and asked to report any questionable calls. If Eleanor and Margaret were anywhere near the Chicago area, the operators may have been able to look up telephone numbers in the metropolitan directory. Then the women could have requested to reverse the charges. Margaret likely had friends in Chicago, in addition to her brother.

Perhaps Eleanor, instead of calling Richard's home, called his sister Hermina. Or she could have contacted Lula, his sister-in-law. Either could have relayed her location to Richard. If Eleanor did have a few dollars, however, another way of making contact would have been to check into an inexpensive hotel and then mail a letter to Richard or one of his family members. The US Postal Service, at the time, was quite efficient and sometimes even delivered mail the same day. If not, a letter would reach the recipient the following day.

Whatever means Eleanor may have used to contact Richard, it's easy to imagine him picking her up and driving her to Lake County. Of his several occupations, the one he listed in the 1940 federal census was "driver, taxicab company." He had the perfect cover to go anywhere, anytime. If Eleanor did, indeed, stay at a rural property, Richard could have relied on his network of confidants who would have checked on her, kept her company, and brought her food during times that Richard couldn't be there.

MARGARET'S TRAIL

Two days after the women's escape, Margaret was thought to have taken a taxi from one suburb of Chicago to another. In "Circle Village in Hunt for Pal of 'Tiger Girl,'" a *Chicago Tribune* reporter wrote:

State and county police and railroad detectives encircled the village of Bensenville, DuPage County, early today in the search for two women who escaped Thursday from the reformatory at Dwight. A taxicab driver, Wiley Taylor, reported he had driven a passenger answering the description of one of the women, Mary Foster, from Franklin Park to Bensenville.

> *The other fugitive is Eleanor Jarman, murderess known as the "blonde tiger girl" because of her vicious treatment of holdup victims. She was believed to be in hiding in Chicago.*
>
> *Taylor told Policeman Elwood Martin of Franklin Park that he became suspicious of his passenger because of her nervous manner and the fact she was undecided where to leave the cab in Bensenville. She wanted to be let out near the railroad. She had paid her fare with a dollar bill. She wore a dress similar to one stolen from a reformatory employee by the fugitives.*
>
> *Mrs. Jarman was serving a 199-year sentence for her part in a holdup slaying, and Miss Foster 1-to-10 years for larceny.*

In addition to the passenger's "nervous manner," the dollar bill cast even more suspicions in the mind of the driver, as Margaret's payment was more than double the fare and tip for the ten-minute drive. If she was the passenger (perhaps in the polka-dotted dress), had she made plans to meet someone at her destination, perhaps someone who could have smuggled her onto an eastbound freight train?

According to a *United Press* article from September 19, 1940, the next place Margaret was thought to have been seen was in Grand Rapids, Michigan. Somehow, after that, she made her way to Springfield, Massachusetts, where she was arrested in November 1940. She had stolen a fur coat from a woman who had employed her for two days as a maid. One has to wonder what Margaret did with all her loot. Did she try to sell it, and, if so, had police checked the local pawn shops?

While Margaret was back in custody, Eleanor, in all likelihood, was safely under the care and protection of Richard and his friends, even as her photograph was sent to law enforcement agencies all over the country. When Massachusetts police were asked about Eleanor, they said they thought that she and Margaret had separated shortly after their escape. Wrote a newspaper reporter at the time, "The trail of Mrs. Jarman was lost from the beginning, and not since her flight have authorities had any trace of her."

CHAPTER 18

Ordinary Woman or "Blonde Tigress"?

ELEANOR WAS FORTUNATE TO HAVE HAD RICHARD SLATER AS HER friend. Did his wife Beaulah know of her husband's former romance and Eleanor and Richard's then-current relationship? Sandra Oliver, his step-granddaughter and now in her seventies, thinks it was very probable. In recent correspondence with the author, she stated that even after Richard's death, Beaulah didn't talk much about him. Sandra added, "It was like there was a deep secret in the family, and it was very well kept."

If Sherlock Holmes, the famed and fictional detective created by author Sir Arthur Conan Doyle, had been consulted on Eleanor's life on the lam, he would have made deductions based on what could be eliminated. There is no hard evidence to substantiate the choices Eleanor made after her escape, but no one, ever again, arrested her, and no one ever found her either dead or alive. If she broke the law, she was not caught, and when she hid in plain sight, she was not recognized. She died under the name of an alias.

The newspaper columnist at the roadblock on the night of her escape, if he was still alive, might now be saying, "Hurrah." After a careful study of Eleanor's past, it becomes evident that she was not the "blonde tigress" that the press had made her out to be. Unlike Margaret who *was* a hardened criminal, Eleanor blended in with ordinary people because she was, in fact, an ordinary woman herself.

FINDING A NEW LOOK

Eleanor's first challenge would have been to modify her appearance. Then she needed to change her identity. With the assumption that Richard or one of his friends brought her groceries, one can imagine her asking for a pair of sharp scissors and a package of bobby pins so she could cut her hair and set it in pin curls for a soft new style. Women's magazines would have given her additional ideas. Eleanor had dyed her hair when she was in hiding with George so, quite possibly, she dyed her hair again. She also may have experimented with wigs, hairpieces, hats, and scarves. She may even have started wearing glasses.

For a complete makeover, Richard's female family members may have donated makeup and fashionable clothes. Perhaps they sent along a couple of pairs of nylon stockings. The synthetic material had been introduced in 1939 at the New York World's Fair. Nylons then became an instant hit with women who preferred their sheerness and cheaper price over the more expensive silk stockings or the heavy cotton ones that Eleanor had to wear in the reformatory. She must have felt like a new woman when she threw away her prison-issued underwear in exchange for dainty store-bought lingerie.

If Richard's small rural retreat had a radio, Eleanor likely enjoyed the Amos 'n' Andy show, still hosting its nightly sitcoms. Then, on Sunday evenings, she may have tuned in to the Jack Benny comedy show. Like Richard, Benny was a Chicago native and the son of Jewish immigrants. On air, no matter what year it was, he claimed to be thirty-nine years old, the same age as Eleanor at the time. Then there were news reports. On August 28, 1940, Eleanor along with other listeners learned that her search had been intensified around Danville, a small town in east-central Illinois. Although nothing came of it, "two women answering the descriptions of the fugitives" were thought to have been seen with a man in a Danville hotel.

When Eleanor was ready to venture outdoors, Richard would have taken her for a drive in his Ford. Perhaps they went to Lake Michigan, then stopped in Lake Forest or one of the other "country towns" to go to a "picture show." A dark movie theater would have been a good place for Eleanor to get used to being around other people without risking exposure. She and Richard may have watched Alfred Hitchcock's psychological thriller *Rebecca*, awarded, in 1940, as the "best picture of the year." Or they could have seen *The Philadelphia Story*, a romantic comedy starring James Stewart, Cary Grant, and Katharine Hepburn. Eleanor had vicariously experienced life on the "outside" on movie nights at the reformatory. But this time, when the film was over, she knew what it was like to be free.

CREATING A NEW IDENTITY

After President Franklin D. Roosevelt's New Deal programs had stabilized parts of the national economy, voters elected him to a third term. One of his programs, the Social Security Act, created a social insurance program designed to pay retired workers sixty-five years or older a continuing income after retirement. Social Security insurance and its requirements hadn't existed before Eleanor was sent to the reformatory.

By 1937, two years after Roosevelt signed the act into law, the federal government had issued more than thirty million Social Security cards in field offices all over the country. Benefits were (and are) based on payroll deductions during a worker's lifetime. Unless Eleanor planned to take day jobs for cash, as Margaret had done, Eleanor would have learned that to find and maintain a steady job she would need a Social Security number and card—obviously in a name other than her own.

According to the Social Security Administration, anyone who applied for a Social Security account at the time had to file a "Form SS-5." Along with one's signature and date, the applicant had eight lines to fill out, as follows:

- Employee's first, middle, and last name
- Street and number, post office, and state
- Business name and address of present employer
- Age at last birthday, date, and place of birth
- Father's and mother's full names
- Sex (male or female)

- Color (white, Negro, other)
- Number on registration card if registered with the US Employment Service
- Then the question, "If you have previously filled out a card like this, state place and date."

In today's world, creating a new identity would be daunting. But in the 1940s (and the 1950s), Social Security clerks generally accepted the information filled in by applicants on their SS-5 forms. These handwritten forms, with little or no verification, simply were filed away. This procedure became evident to the author while doing research on the whereabouts of Twylia May Embrey, an eighteen-year-old who was reported missing in 1952 from North Platte, Nebraska. Many years later, Twylia's siblings were convinced she was dead, as a then recent police investigation had determined that no earnings, ever, had been reported on her Social Security number. The family even had her original card in their possession.

What no one knew the whole time that Twylia was missing was that she had filled out *another* SS-5 form a few years after she left Nebraska. A copy of the form was obtained by the author in 2006 after sending a request, with the name of Twylia's alias, to the Social Security Administration. The alias had been discovered by a fellow researcher who found the then elderly woman's online obituary after Googling only the names of the woman's parents.

Twylia's second SS-5 form also showed that she had falsified additional personal information, including her date and place of birth. After the question that asked whether she had previously filled out a similar form (which she had), Twylia simply checked the box that read "no." After Twylia's death, when a member of her family contacted the obituary's informant, she learned that Twylia, as a teen, had run away and changed her identity because she did not want to be found. Without computers or the Internet, the process had been easy to do.

Eleanor didn't want to be found either. Once she felt confident in her new looks and began to venture out in public, perhaps Richard set her up with her own place to live and a cash-only job. She could have told an employer that she had been abandoned by her husband and had no previous reason to register for Social Security. Then, after proving herself to be a personable and dependable restaurant worker, she would have acquired a reference or two. All she had to do when she was ready to take on a steady job was, like Twylia, go to a Society Security Office and falsify the information on her SS-5 form.

If Eleanor suspected that a clerk might ask for documentation, she could have been prepared with a "delayed birth certificate"—a common affidavit, at the time, signed by an older person "knowledgeable of the date and place of a baby's birth." If that was the case, perhaps someone in Richard's circle of friends stepped in to help. With an alias and a job, Eleanor simply blended into the workforce—the key to her success.

A CHANGING WORLD

Part of Eleanor's reentry into the outside world meant learning to live in the present. Legal bars and saloons had replaced the beer flats and speakeasies of the Prohibition era. If, in the early 1940s, Eleanor served alcoholic drinks, she served them legally for the first time in her adult life. Meanwhile, the country had pulled out of the Great Depression, many people were back at work, and World War II loomed overseas.

News of the war was a common topic of conversation in the United States. Surprisingly, Eleanor and Margaret had some knowledge of Nazi leader Adolf Hitler's 1939 invasion of Poland. According to one of the newspaper reports after the women escaped, they had discussed the plight of Polish refugees with the first of the unsuspecting motorists to give them a ride. They likely had learned of the invasion in one of the reformatory's programs on current events, then brought up the subject so they would appear knowledgeable in the outside world.

In the interim, Italy and Germany had formed an alliance against France and the United Kingdom. German troops invaded France in June 1940, and, in July, the Germans began their bombing (known as the Blitz) of London. At the movies, Eleanor and Richard would have viewed newsreels by commentator Lowell Thomas, as he updated audiences in the short intervals that preceded practically all feature shows.

After December 7, 1941, when the Japanese attacked Pearl Harbor and brought the United States into World War II, women were in high demand in defense industry jobs. Although it's tempting to consider Eleanor working in a munitions factory or related job, the federal government required its workers to be fingerprinted, and her prints already were in their files. Later research suggests that by the time she had obtained her Social Security card, she lived in Missouri. Did Richard keep in contact with her and/or go visit her? No one knows, but he must have been doing well in 1941, as he bought a new car, a Chevrolet special deluxe four-door sedan.

Back at the reformatory, Superintendent Helen H. Hazard ordered the building of a guard tower as a deterrent to further escapes. In December 1941 (more than a year after Margaret was rearrested), a reporter for the Bloomington, Illinois, newspaper wrote that there had been fifty-four escapes in the reformatory's eleven-year history. Without mentioning names, the article indicated that, as of that date, only two had never been found. One was Eleanor. The other, according to a *Chicago Tribune* article in 1953, was Vera Witte, sentenced to life in prison for the murder of her husband. She escaped even earlier than Eleanor, on August 22, 1934. Superintendent Hazard explained that most escapes had been made by "climbing the fence and catching rides to distant points," but only one escape (Eleanor and Margaret's) had been due to carelessness on the part of the staff. That was when Margaret picked the lock while the staff member supposedly guarding them was preoccupied. She subsequently was interrogated and then suspended.

In 1942, two years after her escape, Eleanor did something rather extraordinary. She wrote a letter to her former defense attorney, A. Jefferson Schultze. Her letter must have made quite an impression on the man, as he mentioned it many years later to a *Chicago Tribune* reporter when interviewed about his career. The attorney related that Eleanor had thanked him for saving her from death. The city or town in which the letter was postmarked was not revealed, although Eleanor may have given the sealed envelope to a friend to mail in another city or state to deliberately conceal her location. Nevertheless, the mere fact that she wrote

Figure 18.1. Richard posed in front of his new Chevrolet sedan. Courtesy Sandra Oliver.

the letter showed that she was confident in her situation and secure in her surroundings.

IN THE PUBLIC EYE

Superintendent Hazard of the "State Reformatory for Women, Dwight, Ill." wasted no time printing posters that advertised a reward for Eleanor's apprehension. The posters, with mug shots of Eleanor taken in 1935, were freely distributed and likely displayed in post offices and other public buildings. The reformatory's first poster offered a reward of $50, but it soon was amended to $250, more than $5,000 today. A subsequent poster, also offering $250, was released prior to the April 1943 edition of *Fingerprint and Identification Magazine*. A *Chicago Tribune* article published years later, on July 11, 1993, stated that two of LeRoy's wife's brothers—Paul and Fay Golden, both members of the Sioux City Police Department—vowed to capture Eleanor and collect the money for themselves.

Oddly, the revised poster in the fingerprint magazine had mug shots that showed a younger-looking Eleanor, likely dating from 1933 when Eleanor had been admitted to the institution. The descriptions on both posters were nearly identical, and the one in 1943 read: "Female, age 33 (1933), height 5 ft. 0 in, weight 128, build slight, hair blonde, eyes grey, complexion blonde, conjugal, married, nativity California." The misinformation on her place of birth still had not been corrected from earlier reformatory records. One of Eleanor's mug shots was featured on the publication's cover, along with photographs of seven male offenders. Eleanor's reward was on the high end, as the rewards for the others ranged from $50 to $250.

Although Eleanor's "wanted" status remained in the public eye, her location remained a mystery. *Front Page Detective Magazine* ran a long article in its November 1947 issue titled "Where is the Blonde Tigress?" Accompanying the embellished story was the cheerful photograph of Eleanor (as shown in chapter 5) with the caption, "The 'blonde tigress' smiled sweetly as she went on trial back in 1933. But a Chicago jury couldn't be fooled." The writer began:

Overnight, the attractive blonde turned from a quiet, law-abiding mother of two children into a savage, slugging gun moll. No blind love, no yen for excitement cased this. She was motivated only by a burning desire for money. She combined cunning and stupidity in a manner common to so many outlaws. This caginess, concealed during the seven years she served of her 199-year sentence for murder, enabled her to escape from prison in 1940. "Wanted" circulars on her have been sent all over the country. But she is still free, leading a furtive existence on borrowed time.

After rehashing the stories of robbery victims and the murder of Gustav Hoeh, the writer spoke of Eleanor's time at the reformatory. He even quoted Superintendent Hazard as saying, "She was a willing worker, and no one could have cooperated with us more than she did." Then the article continued:

But in 1940 this changed overnight, and the tigerish factor again dominated Eleanor's character after she met 39-year-old Mary [Margaret] Foster. Mary was a bad apple from way back. She had served two years in the federal penitentiary at Milan, Michigan, for her part in a bank robbery. Her trip to Dwight came in 1939 for a stay of one-to-ten years after she had stolen $10,000 worth of jewelry and clothing from Chicago homes where she had worked as a maid.

Then the writer explained that Mary [Margaret] had made off with $1,000 of an employer's belongings in Grand Rapids, Michigan, before she was arrested and confined in Massachusetts. The story concluded:

Eleanor Jarman did a better job of changing her stripes. From time to time, police received reports that she had been seen in various parts of Illinois, Iowa, Wisconsin, and Michigan, but they never caught up with her. She is still at large. Study her picture and watch for this murderess. A reward of $250 has been offered for her capture by the State of Illinois.

By exploiting Eleanor's story to the hilt, the detective magazine undoubtedly made it easier for an average-looking waitress to fade into the background. After reading the story, though, some readers took it upon themselves to write letters directly to the Federal Bureau of Investigation. These letters were obtained by the author through a Freedom of Information Act (FOIA) request. In the first letter, a resident of Charlotte, North Carolina, explained that he had rented two rooms in his house to a "Mr. and Mrs. Jimmy Martin." Of Mrs. Martin, he stated:

Mrs. Martin acts very nervous and always appears to be afraid of something. She drinks heavily and also appears to be a dope addict. One night I overheard Mr. Martin reprimanding his wife for being so loud, saying that that the folks downstairs would hear her, to which she replied that she did not care and that she would kill all of them.

The Martins had moved to Charlotte from South Carolina, but Mrs. Martin did not have a southern accent. The letter writer added that her hair appeared to have been dyed to a reddish-brown, and that her profile and front view looked exactly like Eleanor's. The resident said he was afraid of her and asked that his identity be kept confidential.

In November 1947, the Washington, DC, office of the FBI received the following letter from a resident of Moscow, Iowa, that read, in part:

I might be mistaken but think I seen this woman [Eleanor Jarman] in Davenport, Iowa. This woman now is about 43–45 years old getting a little heavy, about 5 feet 3 or 4 inches tall, weight about 135–150, hair just turning gray at temples. Has this woman been taken in yet? As to myself, am retired doing nothing but have no use for crooks of any kind. Worked with railroad special offices quite a bit, under cover, but they let out what I was doing and came near being bumped off. Don't let out in any way that I am corresponding with the FBI. There is a bunch here in this part that look funny to me. I do not trust these local police unless I know them all.

FBI Director J. Edgar Hoover (or one of his clerks) responded directly to the Iowa letter writer on November 22, 1947. "The individual to whom you refer is *not* wanted by this Bureau," he stated, "but may be identical with Eleanor Jarman who is wanted by the State Reformatory authorities, Dwight, Illinois. I have taken the liberty of making the information you furnished available to the Warden of the State Reformatory for Women at Dwight, Illinois."

In May 1950, a discharged reformatory inmate was rearrested in Chicago for robbery. Perhaps in the hopes of a plea bargain, the young woman bragged to police that she knew the whereabouts of Eleanor Jarman. The police questioned her further but didn't learn anything new other than the fact that Eleanor had remained a topic of conversation a decade after her escape.

GANG BUSTERS

Newspapers, magazines, and radio broadcasts kept the American public informed for years, but the dawning of the television era in the 1950s ushered in a new and competitive form of entertainment. Topping them all for sensationalism was the show *Gang Busters* that began in 1952 with a series of half-hour crime dramas. The hard-hitting cops and robbers series, however, had first appeared on the radio in 1936. A half-hour radio version of "The Blonde Tigress" aired on November 22, 1940, only three and one-half months after Eleanor and Margaret's escape. The show's producers must have rushed to bring the excitement to its listeners.

At the time of this writing, the complete televised episode of "The Blonde Tigress" (Series 1, Episode 10) is accessible on the Internet on YouTube. Its script is exactly the same as the radio version. Both portray Eleanor as "a vicious woman with strange green eyes," although her eyes weren't green, nor were they mentioned again during the entire show. Diving into fiction and vastly digressing from the facts, the episode's description reads, "A policewoman goes undercover to infiltrate a gang of armed and dangerous criminals led by a vicious but beautiful blonde." As readers are aware, there was no policewoman involved in Eleanor's capture. But the story attracted a lot of viewers, just as media hype in 1933 had swelled the readership of the *Chicago Tribune*.

One scene that includes some elements of fact, however, shows detectives searching the room of "one of Eleanor's boyfriends." The man, "Thomas Batara," clearly portrays Richard Slater. First there's a scene of an apartment manager. When the cops knock on his door, the man reluctantly lets them in and tells them that "Batara" is a "gentleman." The cops search his room and find Eleanor's photo along with a package of love letters. After the detectives leave, one says, "We picked up Batara easily, tracing him through the post office. The Romeo gave us nothing. We used every legitimate trick. He knew them all."

Then, continuing to deviate from the truth, the undercover policewoman, acting as a tourist, asks "Batara" to show her the sights of Chicago. He ends up taking her out for dinner, then mentions that "his girl, Eleanor Jarman," had jilted him for another man. The policewoman asks to meet her. When they reach the hideout, Eleanor holds the policewoman at gunpoint. What the audience, but not Eleanor, knows is that the policewoman had used lipstick to write the address of the hideout on a compact mirror, then she dumped the mirror in a trash can in the bar where she had been with "Batara." The police found the mirror and rushed to the hideout, just as the policewoman wrestled the gun out of Eleanor's hands. The police then arrest Eleanor, George, and even Leo for murder.

The episode ends with the "Commissioner of the Chicago Police Department" seated at his desk, running his hand over a statue of a tigress. The man then shows one of Eleanor's wanted posters and tells his audience that she prefers large handbags (making it easier to conceal a handgun) and may be armed and dangerous. Anyone with information is asked to call the Chicago Police Department, the Illinois State Reformatory for Women, or the *Gang Busters* program.

CHAPTER 19

Lost in Time

THE *GANG BUSTERS* TELEVISION SHOW FAILED TO MENTION ANY INTER-
est in Eleanor by the Federal Bureau of Investigation. According to a later
Chicago Tribune article, the FBI's Springfield, Illinois, Field Office had
"asked for [a] warrant in 1951 after the escaped prisoner was reported
seen in the area." Sightings, though, rarely amounted to more than wish-
ful thinking on the part of the sighter, and Springfield is only 124 miles
from Dwight. Even if Eleanor was just passing through, it seems unlikely
that she would have been out in public that close to the Oakdale Reformatory. Maybe "the area" included Chicago and/or all of Illinois.

During the early years of the 1950s, everyone, it appears, except the
family, searched for Eleanor. Perhaps they thought of her, though, in
1966, when country singer Merle Haggard released his number one hit
single, "The Fugitive." Audiences cheered when he sang, "Down every
road there's one more city. I'm on the run, the highway is my home."

WANTED BY THE FBI

Although the reformatory had issued several "reward" posters on Eleanor
from the early days after her escape, the FBI didn't issue its first "Wanted"
poster for her until March 2, 1953. What had prompted the FBI's action
at that time was its filing of a complaint on January 31, 1952, accusing
Eleanor of violating Title 18, US Code, Section 1073—the Fugitive
Felon Act. The federal agency's charge was "Unlawful Flight to Avoid
Confinement" or, more specifically, "fleeing the state of Illinois to avoid
confinement after conviction for the crime of murder." But what had led

the FBI to believe that Eleanor had left Illinois? This we'll never know, as a Freedom of Information Act request filed with the FBI only revealed that the agency's routine purging of its files had destroyed Eleanor's records.

Eleanor's FBI Wanted poster included the same mug shots from 1935 that, by 1953, were eighteen years out of date. With nearly two decades to change her hair and having aged in the interim, how could anyone have recognized her? Although Eleanor's age had been updated to fifty-one, the rest of her description read as follows:

Born April 22, 1901, Sioux City, Iowa; Height 5'; Weight 99 to 128 pounds; Build slight; Hair blonde, may be dyed red; Eyes, grey; Complexion, light; Race, white; Nationality, American; Occupation, waitress; Remarks, upper front tooth may be false or missing.

To further publicize the FBI's Wanted poster, *King Features Syndicate*, an agency that sold print coverage to newspapers, published a series of short articles on criminals wanted by the FBI. Again, on April 30, 1953, Eleanor's outdated mug shots and story were splashed across the country. In addition to her basic information, the writer inserted, "She has a flair for fancy, high-heeled shoes." Where did that tidbit of information come from? From the days of her trial, every published photograph of Eleanor that showed her feet also showed her wearing the same basic pair of shoes. If she was working as a waitress in the 1950s, she would have worn something more comfortable than fancy high heels.

The only role that the FBI actively played in its search for Eleanor was from January 31, 1952 (when the agency filed its Fugitive Felon Act), to November 24, 1954, when it dropped its charge against her. At that time, the *Chicago Tribune* published a short article titled "Fugitive Warrant for Woman Slayer Dropped on Request." In the story, a spokesman for the FBI stated that the agency "ran out of leads and desired to clear its dockets." The FBI did specify that the warrant could be reinstated at any time if Eleanor were found. Further correspondence between the FBI and the reward seekers who continued to write in with tips were instructed that the State Reformatory for Women, at Dwight, still maintained its "active wanted notice."

In June 1954, *True Detective* magazine included yet another write-up on Eleanor, with the same outdated mug shots, but the reward had been reduced from $250 to $100. Another magazine, *Crime Detective*, in January 1958, again told her story. In response, the FBI (even though it no longer was looking for her) received additional letters with more possible sightings that ranged from Portland, Maine, to Winnipeg, Manitoba. But none led to her arrest.

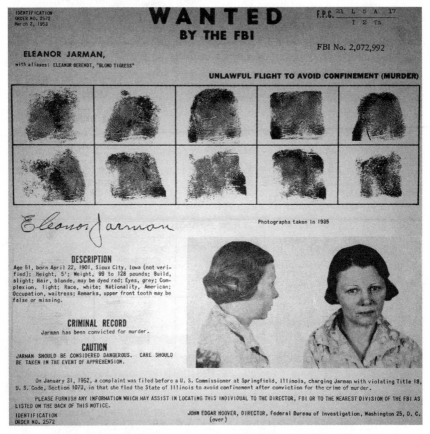

Figure 19.1. Eleanor's FBI Wanted poster stated that she had "fled the state of Illinois." FBI, public domain.

Past Partners

As revealed in chapter 17, Eleanor's escape partner, Margaret Keringer (known at the reformatory as Mary Foster) was arrested in Springfield, Massachusetts, in November 1940. A court ruling then sent her to the Cincinnati Workhouse where she previously had been incarcerated. Authorities managed to keep her locked up until 1945. Then, specifying that she could serve her federal sentence concurrently with her charges in Illinois, they transferred her back to the Oakdale Reformatory, in Dwight. No doubt the other inmates questioned her about life on the run and about Eleanor.

As specified in Margaret's reformatory records, she attempted to escape again after five months, but she was not successful. Perhaps she was spotted by a guard in the reformatory's then new guard tower. Margaret formally was discharged on September 30, 1949. Normal procedure at the time was for Superintendent Helen Hazard to give the released inmate a suitcase with three dresses and pajamas, all made by inmates, along with a store-bought coat and store-bought underwear. The former inmate also was given ten dollars (more than $200 today) and a bus ticket to her chosen destination. If Margaret received the same, she was much better equipped than she and Eleanor had been when they climbed over the fence with the blue suit and the polka-dotted dress.

In the early 1950s, Margaret lived freely in New York where she obtained a Social Security number and card under her married name, with the spelling of Margaret Mackeron. Her estranged husband, Jack, however, had assumed the identity of a younger brother and moved to Ventura, California. According to a family descendant, Jack changed his name to John Charles Curtis, no doubt to escape some of his own past criminal activities. "John" then remarried and raised a second family of seven children. Meanwhile, his four children from his first marriage were scattered across the country in foster homes. By that time, Margaret had moved to Palm Beach, Florida, where she lived with her brother John Keringer and died in 1973. Her body was transported to New York and buried as Margaret Keringer Mackeron next to her sister Julia and husband in the Holy Mount Cemetery in Westchester County, New York.

Just as there is no known record for a divorce between Margaret and her husband, there is no known record for a divorce between Eleanor and her long-estranged husband, Michael Roy Jarman. As previously noted, he and his second wife, Edna, moved from Chicago to Muscatine, Iowa, where they raised their family, a second family for Michael Roy. By the mid-1940s, the Jarmans had moved to San Francisco, California. According to the 1950 federal census, Edna worked as a maid in a hospital, but Michael Roy was unemployed at the time. His whereabouts after that are a mystery. In recent years, Robert James Jarman (a now deceased grandson from Michael Roy's second marriage) noted on the genealogical website Ancestry.com, "He [Michael Roy Jarman] walked out of the house, not in good health, drinking excessively, and was never heard from again."

Eleanor's partners from her crime days were George Dale and Leo Minneci. If Eleanor had picked up a newspaper in August 1957, she might have read that Leo had been paroled from prison. Like Eleanor, he, too, had received a 199-year sentence, but he was released, at the age of fifty, after serving twenty-four years. The main reason, in addition to good behavior, was Leo's participation in World War II malaria "experiments," or what we would today call clinical trials. At the time, American soldiers overseas were dying from the mosquito-spread disease, and the federal government desperately needed to test various treatments. Inmates who volunteered for the experiments were rewarded with cash and shortened sentences. Participating inmates received injections of blood from specially bred and infected mosquitos. Many in the public considered the treatments ethically questionable, as some were known to be toxic. Leo obviously survived, as he lived the last fourteen years of his life as a free man, back in Chicago. He died in 1971 at the age of sixty-four.

If Eleanor had not been caught up in her romance with George, it's not likely that she would have become involved in crime. Without Margaret, it was not likely that Eleanor would have escaped. As for Michael Roy, he was the father of her children. A careful study of Eleanor's life shows Richard Slater as the "partner" who had the most influence. From 1940, when Eleanor escaped, and likely through the early 1950s, Richard helped her successfully blend into society. Considering all that we know of each of them, and Richard's description in the reformatory records as Eleanor's "very close friend," their continued relationship seemed guaranteed.

Throughout the 1940s, not much seemed to have changed in Richard's life. He and Beaulah continued to visit their Lake County retreat, and Beaulah's daughter (Richard's stepdaughter) grew up and married. The Slaters, however, still lived at 4660 Broadway, where Richard was known to hide silver dollars for visiting grandchildren. According to the 1950 federal census, Beaulah took a job in a radio factory, while Richard listed his occupation as bartender.

As in previous years, Richard had kept up with his gambling interests. His only known conflict with the law was in 1949 when he was one of thirty-four people involved in two poker games in a Veterans of Foreign Wars clubhouse. According to the *Chicago Tribune*, the Chicago police raided the building and booked nineteen women and ten men, then identified the remaining five as "keepers and dealers." One was "Richard Slater, 49, of 4660 Broadway." Back in gang leader Jack Zuta's time, the mobster's account books reflected payoffs to the police. Had that happened this time as well? Richard and his cohorts were released on bond.

In late 1954 (the same year that the FBI dropped its warrant on Eleanor), Richard and Beaulah moved from Chicago to Louisville, Kentucky, where Beaulah had lived in the 1930s. There was some talk in the family of them having to leave Chicago in a hurry. In Louisville, the couple bought and operated a business, the Sea-Cal Cleaners. Richard also hosted poker games in the back room of a used car dealership. As Sandra Oliver, his step-granddaughter, remembers, "Most grandfathers teach their grandkids how to fish or read a book. Nope. Mine taught me how to bet on a horse. Now, that's a memory."

Sandra adds that she loved him very much. Richard died in Louisville in 1968, and whether he had kept in contact with Eleanor in his later years is not known. According to family lore, "he died in the arms of another woman."

REQUEST FOR CLEMENCY

Eleanor's son LeRoy, after his undisclosed absence following his term in the Civilian Conservation Corps, returned to Sioux City. There, in 1941, he married Ruby Elaine Golden before entering the Army in 1942. The couple's home, however, remained in Sioux City where they raised their two sons, Daniel and Douglas. While LeRoy was in the Army, LaVerne joined the Navy. He married his first wife in Iowa, then moved to Florida where he remained for most of the rest of his life. Eleanor, whether she knew it or not, had become a grandmother.

Both sons were opposed to searching for Eleanor. As LeRoy later was quoted as saying, he feared that any publicity would expose the family to ridicule, tarnish their businesses, and lead to possible arrests. His younger son Douglas, however, didn't agree. Three months after LeRoy's unexpected death on March 1, 1993, Douglas filed a "Petition for Commutation of Sentence on Behalf of Eleanor Jarman" with the Illinois Prisoner Review Board. The *Associated Press* later reported, "LeRoy Jarman's death was the catalyst for the family campaign."

Douglas then hired well-known attorney David P. Schippers, who had formerly served as Chicago Chief of Organized Crime in the US Attorney General's Office. Douglas addressed his petition to Illinois governor James Edgar and submitted it to the Review Board pursuant to 730 ILCS 5/3–313 of the Illinois Compiled Statutes. In his supporting documentation, Douglas outlined Eleanor's crime, sentence, and escape, then contended that she had been "unduly convicted and punished for the crime of another." In his argument, he wrote, in part, "At the time of her arrest, she was working as a waitress and was still considered married to the man who had abandoned her with her two young children. The crime of which she was convicted was the only blot on her record." Then he added:

> Since her escape, her family has not been in contact with her [author's emphasis]. However, the family has reason to believe that Ms. Jarman is still alive, is living outside of the State of Illinois, and has lived an exemplary life since her escape from the Dwight Correctional Institution [formerly Oakdale Reformatory] fifty-three years ago. Although

it is impossible to state at this time in any great detail the type of life that the Petitioner has led since her escape, it is obvious that she has never been arrested or otherwise come to the attention of law enforcement officials. It can therefore be assumed that she has been peaceful and law-abiding for at least the last fifty years.

In his document, Douglas asked for a commutation of Eleanor's sentence up to time served. "It is her grandson's hope," he wrote, "to finally meet the grandmother that he has never known and to share memories of his deceased father with her. He also hopes to introduce his children to their great-grandmother while she is still alive. In addition, the other son [LaVerne Jarman] of the Petitioner Eleanor Jarman, is still living and hopes to meet with his mother one last time." Douglas continued:

So long as the Petitioner is still under sentence and is considered a wanted fugitive, it will be virtually impossible for the family to meet, or even to find her. Ms. Jarman has served seven years in jail for being with the wrong people at the wrong time; and has been effectively in exile, away from her family, for an excess of another fifty years. She has been punished enough and has long since paid her debt to society. At this point, the only compassionate and decent thing to do is to try to unite the Jarman family.

Douglas's take on Eleanor's murder charge—that she had been with the wrong people at the wrong time—is reminiscent of Superintendent Hazard's opinion that women involved in murder usually acted under the bad influences of men.

The chairman of the Prisoner Review Board quickly replied and stated that Douglas's petition was not complete and did not conform to board requirements. The board did, however, schedule the petition for a hearing in the fall of 1993, providing that Douglas and attorney Schippers send an amended petition by September. On their second attempt, the men filled in some gaps, but they neglected to research Eleanor's prison years, and they didn't check at the Woodbury County Courthouse, in Sioux City, for the correct date and place of "Ella's" birth.

A sentence in Douglas's amended petition that did not meet the board's approval read, "Prior to this Petition, no other requests for Executive Clemency have ever been made by Eleanor Jarman or by anyone else on her behalf." The chairman, whose staff did do its research, replied, "Our files disclose that she [Eleanor Jarman] petitioned Governor Henry Horner for executive clemency on June 15, 1935, and was denied by the Governor on October 23, 1935." The June 1935 petition (although its date is a few days earlier than in the reformatory's records) was the one for which Richard Slater's family, along with Eleanor's coworker and her children's doctor, had written letters attesting to her character.

In bolstering Douglas's claim that the family "had reason to believe" that Eleanor was still alive, he stated in his amended petition:

> *Her family, however, is aware, based on authority in which they place trust and confidence, that after her escape Eleanor Jarman worked as a waitress or as a hostess in various restaurants outside the State of Illinois. For approximately the past 20 years, she has been employed and has been living on her savings and probably Social Security.*

On September 20, 1993, the Prisoner Review Board denied Douglas's Amended Petition, as the board's chairman objected to being forced to "accept speculation or vague assurances from an 'authority.'" He also wrote that he found it "troubling to be asked to wink at her [Eleanor's] status as a fugitive."

FAMILY STORIES

In between Douglas's first and amended petitions, he met with several reporters, including John O'Brien of the *Chicago Tribune*. In his first interview, Douglas talked freely about the contacts that Eleanor's family *did* have with her. This was less than a month after he claimed in his first petition to the Prisoner Review Board that his family had *not* been in contact with her. In the amended petition, he didn't admit or deny any contact.

Douglas's interview with O'Brien was published on July 11, 1993. According to Douglas, his father, LeRoy, had told him that he had corresponded with Eleanor in a rather unusual way—via classified advertisements in various out-of-state newspapers, including the *Kansas City Star*. Both Eleanor and LeRoy were said to have used aliases and, supposedly, exchanged simple phrases such as "Let's have coffee" that meant something unique just to them. When, and if, these coded messages were sent back and forth is not known, nor has their existence been publicly confirmed.

For LeRoy, in Sioux City, to have inserted a paid advertisement in another city's newspaper, he would have mailed his written message along with cash or a check. Eleanor could have done the same from anywhere in the country. According to Douglas's interviews, Eleanor never disclosed her location, although she did say that she worked in restaurants, as she had done for most of her life.

Another piece of family lore that also surfaced in the *Tribune*'s July 1993 article was relayed to the reporter by then-ninety-three-year-old Dorothy Berendt, wife of Eleanor's brother Otto Berendt. According to Dorothy, she and Otto met Eleanor, in person, at a bus station in Sioux City, Iowa, in 1975. According to Dorothy, Eleanor had arrived on a Greyhound bus. As Dorothy told the reporter:

> *I was looking around the bus station for her because that is where she said on the phone she would be. A voice in the shadows said, "Are you looking for somebody?" I said I was, and the voice replied, "Could be me you are looking for." That's when Ella [Eleanor] Jarman stepped forward.*
>
> *She was relaxed and looked pretty good. Still the same woman I had known. We got in the car and Otto drove out to Isaac Walton Lake to talk. All she wanted to know was if her boys were okay. We told her they were grown men and doing good for themselves.*

The reporter then added that during the lakeside chat, a police car appeared, and its driver looked over the trio—the only people parked by the lake. Otto and Dorothy stiffened, but Eleanor, according to Dorothy, "didn't blink an eye." Instead she said, "Relax. The police stopped looking for me years ago." After her visit with Otto and Dorothy, Eleanor met back in Sioux City with her son LeRoy. Although she still refused to tell her family where she lived, she said, "I have a lot of friends where I am at. They know the true story."

Dorothy's mention of arrangements being made by phone begs the question as to how often Eleanor had talked on the phone with Dorothy or anyone else in her family. Decades after Eleanor's escape, was the family concerned that their phone was being tapped? Another unanswered question is a more obvious one. Dorothy claimed no knowledge of where Eleanor had come from, but a simple inquiry at the bus station would at least have told her if the bus had pulled in from the east or west, as well as its place of origin.

Between Douglas's original and amended petitions to the review board, there had been a lot of interest by movie-goers in the release of the film *The Fugitive*, starring Harrison Ford. Fugitives were a hot topic, and Douglas was asked to be a guest on the television program *CBS This Morning*. He also appeared on *Hard Copy*, a "tabloid show" that, according to the online encyclopedia Wikipedia "was aggressive in its use of questionable material." Douglas's interview, shown to a nation-wide audience on August 17, 1993, was titled "Man Searches for Outlaw Grandma." He likely told the show's viewers what he had told the newspaper reporters—that he believed Eleanor was alive because, in Eleanor's 1975 visit to Sioux City, she told LeRoy she would arrange for someone to notify him when she died.

During this same time, the celebrity tabloid *Star Magazine* ran a story titled "Have You Seen This 93-Year-Old Killer Granny?" with the subtitle "Blonde Tigress Has Been on the Lam for 53 Years—Now Family Wants to Find Her." After reminding the magazine's readers that Eleanor was "the most dangerous woman in America," its writer asked for tips to be sent to the *National Enquirer*. According to the files of the Illinois Prisoner Review Board, there weren't any replies. The detective magazine days, as well as "sightings" of Eleanor, were over.

The extensive publicity, however, spread all over the country. In California, it reached Pat DeOliveira, one of the daughters of Eleanor's son LaVerne. Pat was only eight years old when she first learned about Eleanor from a brother, but she didn't tell anyone. In an interview with the author, she stated:

When Doug Jarman petitioned for clemency, I was about 46, and the story, with Eleanor's photo, was in the local newspaper. My kids and grandkids were gathered at my home playing games in the yard when my older son came out with the paper. He said, "Mom, I know you can't be related, but I saved this paper because she [Eleanor] looks just like you." We were all shocked! We talked about it and of course they wanted more.

Meanwhile, the *Chicago Tribune* reporter had tracked down two grandsons of murder victim Gustav Hoeh. When asked their opinions of Douglas's clemency petition, one grandson stated, "I'd just as soon they leave alone what was left forgotten." The other grandson replied, "It was a vicious crime. As I understand the details, she [Eleanor] played an active part. Even if it had been a minor role, she would get no mercy from me."

In June 1994, Douglas released to the press a letter his family had recently received—supposedly from Eleanor—stating that she was alive, had married, and had inherited a considerable sum of money. Questions arose as to whether the letter could have been a hoax. A reporter for the *Sioux City Journal* even stated that "experts" had found fingerprints on the letter and determined they were a close match to Eleanor's, taken when she entered the reformatory. If that had been the case, the Sioux City Police Department or another law enforcement agency surely would have confirmed the startling find.

Regardless as to the letter's authenticity, it was said to have been mailed from Des Moines, Iowa, and claimed that Eleanor was living in a nursing home. This was before the common use of the Internet, so Douglas physically traveled to Des Moines where he visited nursing homes, searched telephone directories, and combed through marriage records, but he didn't find Eleanor.

In December 1994, more than a year after the Review Board had turned down Douglas's Amended Petition, *Chicago Tribune* reporter John

O'Brien wrote another article titled "Hunt for Blonde Tigress nearing end for grandson." In the interview, Douglas revealed the name that his father had told him that Eleanor had taken for herself—Marie Mellman or Marie Millman. As for Douglas, he said he had ideas and plans. "Sometime in my lifetime," he added, "I'm going to find out."

Chapter 20

Tables Turned

Douglas Jarman died in 1999, at the age of fifty-one. Had he lived longer, he may well have found Eleanor, but he had no way, at the time, of searching Eleanor's aliases in other parts of the country. In 2021, after the author read that Eleanor was believed to be the longest-running missing female fugitive in the country, she decided to pick up the challenge. The first, and biggest, step was to compile as much information as possible about Eleanor, then insert her life experiences into historical context and try to figure out what she thought and how she felt about herself and the events in her life. As award-winning author Anne Lamott wrote in her book *Bird by Bird: Some Instructions on Writing and Life* (Random House, 1994), writers only need to focus on their characters, and the plot will take care of itself. Solving a missing person or missing fugitive case uses the same philosophy. Investigators call it following the evidence.

Evidence on Eleanor

The author received the assistance of two invaluable fellow researchers who each dug deeply and followed their own intuitions. When everyone's facts were compiled and combined with new insights, the following points became clear:

- As the tenth child in a large family, especially after the death of her mother, Eleanor learned to depend on her siblings. She was a follower, not a leader.

- During the early days of the Great Depression, Eleanor was a single mother with two small children. She provided for herself and them as a waitress—work that she claimed she had done since the age of twelve.

- Eleanor continued to work while she lived with Richard Slater. During the winter of 1932–1933, after she lost her then recent waitress job, she met George Dale, a store robber who helped her with money for rent. Eleanor began to accompany him, then continued at his side possibly to keep his affections.

- Eleanor had been brought up in a law-abiding family and knew that she was responsible for her actions. However, hunger, hormones, or even the survival of her children kept her entangled with George.

In the reformatory, in interview after interview, Superintendent Helen Hazard called Eleanor a "model prisoner." There, too, she was a follower—following the institution's rules and then following Margaret right over the fence. Once on the "outside," Eleanor relied on her intelligence to contact Richard, the best-positioned person to help her. After she acquired a new look and a new identity, she had the confidence to do the only job she knew how to do—wait on tables.

When did Eleanor take control of her life and really begin to feel free? Perhaps it was when Richard got her settled in the rural retreat, or when he first took her out in public. Or maybe it was the first time she walked the streets of Chicago or some other city and realized she was only one small person in a big crowd, and she could do whatever she wanted with the rest of her life.

It's easy to imagine Eleanor rationalizing her freedom. George had pulled the trigger, and he paid with his life. Eleanor and Leo each were sentenced to 199 years—sentences that the Illinois Parole and Pardon Board later admitted were "unduly severe." Eleanor had been in the wrong place at the wrong time, and, yes, she had committed a crime or crimes. But she spent seven years in the reformatory where, some would argue, she paid her debt to society. She had served her time.

A WAITRESS IN DENVER

When Merle Haggard sang, "Down every road there's one more city," Eleanor already had found her new home. After weighing all the evidence, it is the author's belief that Eleanor spent her last twenty-nine years working as a waitress in the area on and near Colfax Avenue in Denver, Colorado. Like Madison Street in Chicago, Colfax Avenue is a main east-west thoroughfare through a major American city. Madison Street runs between Lake Michigan and what used to be open prairies, while Colfax Avenue (on its eastern end) extends from former prairie land to the abrupt uplift of the Rocky Mountains. In both Chicago's and Denver's early settlement days, both streets were lined with quiet residential neighborhoods. Then, in the 1920s and 1930s, the residential areas evolved into commercial strips of lunchrooms, diners, corner groceries, and other small shops and businesses.

In Chicago, Eleanor had worked in three or four small restaurants in the Garfield Park neighborhood. All were close to her first apartment on West Madison Street. Then, according to Denver City directories (accessible via Ancestry.com), the waitress the author believes to have been Eleanor was employed by similar small restaurants on Colfax Avenue. She began her work in Denver in 1951 and retired in 1974. One can easily picture her, then middle aged, walking to work in her comfortable shoes and showing up on time with a smile on her face.

Under her alias, Eleanor lived openly, day after day, serving her patrons the "early bird special" or whatever they ordered, as she never left the lunch counter for other types of work. She was steadily employed, so she must have gotten along well with her employers and staff. She would have chatted with the "regulars" and commiserated with those down on their luck. Her coworkers and her neighbors were her friends, and it's easy to believe that her life was good.

Back in the 1940s, after Eleanor's escape from the reformatory, there can be little room for doubt that Richard had come to her aid. Similarly, in a search for Eleanor's later whereabouts, it only makes sense that she would take up a familiar line of work in a similar setting. In addition, an alias of "Marie" was a logical choice as Eleanor was known as Ella Marie Berendt as a child. Accessing the genealogical databases Ancestry.com and FamilySearch.org, along with the historical newspaper databases Newspapers.com and NewspaperArchive.com, the author searched all appropriate women with the names "Marie Mellman" and "Marie Millman" (as Douglas Jarman had suggested) everywhere in the country.

Initial Research

These names were narrowed down to those similar in age to Eleanor. Necessary to keep in mind, however, is that people who don't want to be found will falsify their birth dates. Eleanor's estimated age, therefore, had to fit into a date range rather than a specific year.

Then came the question as to whether "Millman" or "Mellman" was a maiden or married name. Assuming the former, all women with parents and/or siblings were discarded, as an assumed name couldn't have documented relatives. Also culled from the list, in case of a married name, were those with marriage and/or divorce records. Obituaries were helpful too in determining if a "Marie" had parents, a spouse, siblings, or children. A check of the federal 1940 census was invaluable in eliminating even more names, as Eleanor herself had been listed in the census at the Oakdale Reformatory, four months before her escape. Obviously, she couldn't have been Eleanor and Marie at the same time.

After eliminating the impossible, as Sherlock Holmes would have done, the only remaining candidate was a Marie Millman—the waitress in Denver. She was a perfect fit, as extensive genealogical research confirmed that she had no parents, siblings, husbands, or children. Denver City directories, however, did provide eighteen listings that showed her residential and work addresses beginning in 1951 and continuing through 1979. Marie lived alone in a series of apartment buildings, and she worked nearby in small restaurants that included The Kitchen (later, Pete's Kitchen), Super Chef, and Sam's Cafe. Pete's Kitchen, at 1962 East Colfax Avenue, is the only one of these businesses still in existence.

An additional piece of information that shows up on Ancestry.com is a transcription of Marie Millman's Social Security Death Index, stating that she was born May 4, 1908 (the date she would have supplied in her now-missing application), and died in August 1980. As the author had done during her search for Twylia May Embrey (see chapter 18), she

Figure 20.1. In 1959 and 1960, Marie Millman worked at Pete's Kitchen, formerly The Kitchen. At the time, she lived around the corner at 1457 Vine Street, in Denver, Colorado. Photo in 2021 by the author.

sent off for Marie's Form SS-5 from the Social Security Administration. Not only was it missing, but also missing was Marie's name in the Social Security Claims and Application Index, indicating that no one had filed for her death benefit, as a family member normally would do after a death.

The author did, however, receive a Request for Earnings Record for "Marie H. Millman," confirming Marie's last-known address of Apartment 14, 330 East 16th Avenue, Denver, Colorado. The Death Index document also stated that Marie's Social Security number of 500–14–3792 had been issued "before 1951" in Missouri. According to Douglas Jarman, in a 1993 newspaper interview, his father LeRoy Jarman claimed that when he and Eleanor corresponded via classified ads, one of the newspapers was the *Kansas City Star*, from Kansas City, Missouri.

The year 1951, when Marie Millman first showed up in Denver, also was the year that the FBI filed its complaint stating that Eleanor had "fled the state of Illinois." Was there a connection? We'll never know, as a Freedom of Information/Privacy Act (FOIPA) request for any information on Marie Millman was returned with the simple statement, "We were unable to identify records responsive to your request."

POSTMORTEM

Because initial research on Marie Millman showed her to be a good candidate for Eleanor's alias, the author set up a private research "tree" on Ancestry.com to keep track of dates, addresses, places of employment, and all other relevant data. After more than a year of searching, absolutely nothing new showed up prior to 1951. If Eleanor previously had used the name "Marie Millman," she was careful not to leave a paper trail.

The next step was to see what, if any, records existed for Marie Millman after her death. In response to a request to the Denver Probate Court, the author received Marie's twenty-five-page probate file. Marie died on August 14, 1980, intestate, that is, without a will. Shortly afterward, the probate court assigned Marie's estate a personal representative, identified in the documentation as the "petitioner." More than a year after Marie's death, the probate court's final settlement read:

Petitioner, after diligent inquiry and search, has not been able to locate, or determine, the existence of any heir, or heirs, of the decedent and believes that any further search or inquiry would be of no avail, and the assets of the estate should escheat to the State of Colorado pursuant to 15–12–914 of the Colorado Probate Code.

The petitioner paid himself a hefty sum, as he was permitted to do, and he also used Marie's bank account at the Western Federal Savings Bank to pay off her other expenses. Included was the cost of an ambulance that took Marie from her apartment to Denver's Saint Joseph Hospital, where she spent eight days before she died. If she was Eleanor, she was seventy-nine years old. After all of her bills were paid, the state of Colorado claimed Marie's remaining estate of $4,469.49, worth more than $16,000 today.

On August 18, 1980, the Capitol Mortuary, in Denver, published a brief newspaper notice that read, "Marie Millman, late of Denver, Arrangements later, Chapel of the Chimes." A careful search through subsequent newspapers, however, failed to show any "later" arrangements, and the mortuary had no records from that time period. Although there was no mention of a funeral or service, the probate file did show a $25 "funeral expense" paid to Carl Davidson, a Methodist pastor.

Marie was interred in Denver's Fairmount Cemetery on August 22, 1980. Perhaps the pastor spoke a few words at her grave. Hopefully, Marie's neighbors and coworkers also attended. The author has visited her grave, as well, in block 67, section 5, lot 540, near the perimeter of the historic cemetery's carefully maintained grounds. A modest flat stone marks the site. Those of us who have come to know and care for Eleanor/Marie can rest assured that she was cared-for and at peace.

DISHING OUT CHILI

If Eleanor was Marie, what had brought her to Denver? Often, people move to a place recommended by family or friends. Eleanor's only known family connection to Denver was through her sister-in-law Dorothy Berendt. She and her husband Otto were the couple who had secretly met with Eleanor in Sioux City in 1975 (see chapter 19). Dorothy, however,

Figure 20.2. Marie Millman's flat gravestone is among other marked graves in Fairmount Cemetery, in Denver, Colorado, in the "block" identified by curbside marker number "67." Photo in 2021 by author.

had lived and worked as a waitress in Denver in the early 1930s, during a previous marriage. Eleanor's son LeRoy lived with Dorothy and Otto at the time of Eleanor's escape. Perhaps LeRoy, in his coded messages to his mother, suggested Denver as a place to live.

In making sense of Eleanor's untold story, it's important to reflect on who she was as a woman. She had entered the workplace with a below-average education, but her reformatory records indicated an above-average IQ. After her escape with Margaret, while riding in the car with the unsuspecting motorist, Eleanor likely was the one who steered the conversation toward the rumblings of war rather than be confronted with small talk such as "where do you live and what do you do?" At the time of her trial, most of her photos show her looking frightened and subdued, despite her reputation as the notorious "blonde tigress." After her escape, if she hadn't matured into a confident woman, she wouldn't have survived.

Figure 20.3. Marie's gravestone reads, "Marie H. Millman, 1908–1980." The "H" is the same as on her Social Security Earnings Report. Photo in 2021 by author.

Eleanor, as Marie, blended into society as an ordinary working woman, just as she had been before the crime spree that ended in the shopkeeper's murder. Yes, she had joined up with the wrong people at the wrong time, but she wasn't the killer. Nor had she kicked the dying man on the ground.

She served seven years in the reformatory for being an accomplice to murder, then she fulfilled the reformatory's mission—"to return unfortunate girls and women to society, clean, healthful, and with character reconstructed." If Superintendent Hazard had known of Eleanor's law-abiding life and success in her job, she would have, secretly, been proud. For Eleanor, the tables had turned. She wasn't the blonde tigress after all, and she was left with her freedom. She had earned it.

Any of us who were born before 1980 may have passed Eleanor—as Marie—on the street or been served by her in a restaurant. The columnist Ed Lahey, whose wife drove him through Dwight, Illinois, on the night of Eleanor's escape, thought so too. In 1966 he wrote, "When I am in some wayside diner late at night, and a beat-up old doll in her sixties is dishing out chili, I am tempted to ask if she is Eleanor. But I never do."

Lahey ended his column, in part, by adding, "I keep hoping that she got some good out of life. . . . Goodnight, Eleanor Jarman, wherever you are."

ACKNOWLEDGMENTS

First of all, I am deeply indebted to my fellow researchers, Micki Lavigne and Mary Combs. I met Micki online, in 2002, when she answered my genealogical query on "Boulder Jane Doe," a murder victim from 1954. Our combined efforts, in partnership with police and forensic experts, led to the young woman's identity. During the search, Micki found another missing woman, Twylia May Embrey. Her falsified Social Security records tie in with a discussion of similar records for Eleanor Jarman.

In 2020, I began corresponding with Mary Combs when I discovered on Ancestry.com that we both shared an interest in yet another missing woman. I kept in contact with both Micki and Mary, and both eagerly joined my search for Eleanor. Our combined investigations turned up a new (to us) major character in Eleanor's life—Richard Slater. Then our research led to his step-granddaughter, Sandra Oliver. Her willingness to share family information, as well as her family photos and research, added immensely to Eleanor's story. Thank you all.

I also wish to thank my editor and publisher, Rick Rinehart, for his faith in me as I tackled what turned out to be a challenging subject. And special thanks go to Jerry Clark and Ed Palattella, authors of several books including *On the Lam: A History of Hunting Fugitives in America* (Rowman & Littlefield, 2019). They read my manuscript, answered my questions, made invaluable suggestions, and wrote the foreword. Thanks, too, go to their editor, Becca Beuer, for putting me in contact with Ed and Jerry. I feel fortunate that our paths have crossed.

Much of the nitty-gritty research for this book depended upon the availability and kindness of others. For part I, Haley Aguirre, Archival Records Clerk at the Sioux City Public Museum, in Sioux City, Iowa, searched her files and made referrals for further research. Meanwhile, Phyllis McMillan, a volunteer with the Woodbury County Genealogical Society, did in-person lookups for me at the Woodbury County (Iowa) Courthouse. A staff member of Sioux City's Parks Department provided information on Berendt family burials in Sioux City's Floyd Cemetery. In addition, I appreciated corresponding with Carol Vivier (also an Ancestry.com user) about her, and Eleanor's, Berendt family ancestors.

While researching George Dale, I exchanged a couple of emails with Ruth Ann Skaggs of the Historic Madison County Museum in George's hometown of Fredericktown, Missouri. To learn about his, Eleanor's, and Leo's charges of murder, accomplice to murder, and robbery, I found myself on the phone with Julius Machnikowski, staff member of the Circuit Court of Cook County, Illinois. When I explained that I was unable to travel to Chicago to view the court records in person, Julius put me in contact with independent researcher Steven J. Wright. He did an excellent job of copying and forwarding multiple case files. I'm also grateful to the Chicago Police Department for its timely fulfillment of my FOIA request on the murder of Gustav Hoeh.

By that time, I had read Marianne Mather and Kori Rumore's book *He Had It Coming: Four Murderous Women and the Reporter Who Immortalized Their Stories*, illustrated with *Chicago Tribune* photographs of female criminals of Eleanor Jarman's era. The book inspired me to inquire about similar high-quality newspaper photos of Eleanor. At first, I was told that they no longer existed, but Tony Dudek, senior account executive of the Tribune Content Agency, went out of his way to arrange for a researcher to locate and then digitize the requested photographs and make them available to me.

Ellen Keith, director of research and access, and her staff at the Chicago History Museum kindly looked up Chicago addresses for me in city directories and found, in their collections, additional images from the *Chicago Sun Times* and the *Chicago Daily News*.

For part II, I relied heavily on the files from the Circuit Court of Cook County, as well as two extensive Illinois Supreme Court documents provided to me by Eowyn Montgomery, records archivist at the Illinois State Archives in Springfield, Illinois. Eowyn went out of her way to help me, even turning up documents that I hadn't asked for but that proved invaluable.

When I began to research part III and delved into Eleanor's years at the Oakdale Reformatory, I again relied on Eowyn. Although Eleanor's "prison jacket" was nowhere to be found, Eowyn sent me Eleanor's "Application for Commutation of Parole" from 1935, including letters of support. Eowyn also provided me with the "prison jacket" for Mary Foster (aka Margaret Keringer). I also met (on Ancestry.com) Michael S. Makaron, who freely contributed his family's documents, as well as a photograph of his great aunt Margaret.

To provide historic context on the reformatory during the 1930s, Mary Flott and Kim Drechsel, both from the Dwight Historical Society in Dwight, Illinois, enthusiastically supplied me with newspaper articles, documents, and photographs. Meanwhile, I tried to find the final resting place of George Dale, as a newspaper article placed him in one cemetery, while his death certificate gave the name of another. Although staff members of both the Oakwoods and Oak Lawn cemeteries, in the Chicago area, diligently searched for his elusive records, we still don't know where he was buried.

For part IV, while researching the Civilian Conservation Corps (CCC), I corresponded with Lisa Gardinier, University of Iowa Libraries. Meanwhile, Corey S. Stewart, archivist at the National Archives at St. Louis, Missouri, filled me in on Records of the Selective Service System. In my search for land records in Lake County, Illinois, a Lake County Clerk's employee offered to walk me through the county's online database, but it was so efficient that I easily found the records myself. I also appreciated the files of "sightings" sent to me by the FBI in response to my FOIA request on Eleanor Jarman. When I had more in-depth questions, FBI historian John Fox graciously answered my questions on the phone.

An important piece of primary source documentation necessary for this book was the "Petition for Commutation of Sentence on Behalf of Eleanor Jarman, 1993," obtained through a FOIA request from the Illinois Prisoner Review Board in Springfield, Illinois. I'm grateful to the board's chief legal counsel, Kahalah A. Clay, who completed my request.

I also appreciated several lengthy phone conversations with Jon Seidel, crime reporter at the *Chicago Sun-Times*. In addition to referring me to the Prisoner Review Board, he brainstormed with me about various additional research sources.

When I contacted Michael J. Hancock, archives specialist at the National Archives, for a search of records on Eleanor Jarman at the Department of Justice, he replied, "I actually enjoyed researching your request. It's a very interesting case!" Comments from people like him, a complete stranger, were especially rewarding.

For research on Marie Millman (Eleanor's alias), I contacted the Social Security Administration. The agency provided Marie's Request for Earnings statement and confirmed its lack of any other documentation. The FBI (in response to my FOIA request on Marie) also stated that it had no additional information. It's hard to prove a negative, but the Marie Millman "tree" on Ancestry.com was essential in proving that Marie had no family.

Then, after the Denver, Colorado, Probate Office fulfilled my request for Marie's probate file, the final pieces of the puzzle fell into place—the file confirmed that Marie had no known heirs. The Probate Office also provided Marie's place of burial in Denver's Fairmount Cemetery. I appreciated the kind staff member who directed me to her grave.

Last, I thoroughly enjoyed my correspondence with Pat DeOliveira, one of Eleanor's granddaughters. May this book answer some of her, and her family's, questions.

FOR FURTHER READING

An online search for fugitives led the author to Eleanor Jarman's name and brief biography, followed by dozens of sensationalized and conflicting newspaper reports. Serious researchers, however, are well aware that they need to seek out *primary* sources of information to fully document their characters. Only then is one prepared to speculate on an individual's thoughts, feelings, and life choices. But where does the research begin?

The author started by creating a private "Eleanor Berendt Research Tree" on the genealogical website Ancestry.com. After entering Eleanor's basic data, the facts of her life were fleshed out with the names of family members and associates, as well as census records and life events obtained from both online and offline sources. The tree grew into an outline that motivated the author to search for primary source (and mostly offline) documents. The most prominent of these sources, in order of use, included:

- "Report #5160, Murder of Gustav Hoeh." Department of Police, City of Chicago, Chicago, Illinois, 1933.

- *People vs. Eleanor Jarman et al*, 1933, specifically CR-70149 (murder) and CR-70150 through CR-70155 (robbery). Circuit Court of Cook County.

- *The People of the State of Illinois vs. George Dale, otherwise known as George Kennedy; Eleanor Jarman, and Leo Minneci*, Supreme Court of the State of Illinois, December Term A.D. 1933. Illinois State Archives.

- *The People of the State of Illinois vs. George Dale, otherwise known as George Kennedy; Eleanor Jarman, and Leo Minneci—Brief and Argument for Plaintiff in Error.* Supreme Court of the State of Illinois, April Term A.D. 1934, Illinois State Archives. (This is a separate document from the previous one.)
- "Application for Commutation of Parole for Eleanor Jarman, 1935," Illinois State Archives. (This includes the letters from Richard Slater's family members.)
- Mary Foster's (aka Margaret Keringer's) "prison jacket" from Dwight Reformatory, 1940. Illinois State Archives.
- Grantor Index 1936–1957 and related property records for Richard and Beaulah Slater. Recorder of Deeds Office of Lake County, Illinois.
- Federal Bureau of Investigation correspondence regarding Eleanor Jarman, number #2072992. FBI Freedom of Information Act (FOIA) Request. (These are letters regarding possible "sightings.")
- "Petition for Commutation of Sentence on Behalf of Eleanor Jarman," 1993. Illinois Prisoner Review Board.
- "Petition for Final Settlement and Distribution in the Matter of the Estate of Marie Millman, Probate Number 80-PR-1207," 1981. Denver Probate Court.

Additional online sources widely used throughout the book included FamilySearch.org, FindAGrave.com, Google Search, Google Maps, Newspapers.com, and NewspaperArchive.com. Newspaper reports are secondary sources and often contain errors, but they are helpful when constructing timelines. They also can provide insights such as colorful details and quotes that make people in the stories come alive.

A NOTE ON ELEANOR'S "PRISON JACKET"
Although the Illinois State Archives has many inmate records (called "prison jackets") from the Oakdale Reformatory, Eleanor's—number 692—at the time of this writing is missing. To fill in the gap, the author

reconstructed her file by drawing from the Illinois Supreme Court documents, from Eleanor's 1935 Application for Commutation of Parole, and from the 1993 Petition for Commutation of Sentence. According to a notation in the Prisoner Review Board's file, Eleanor's "jacket" was still at the reformatory (renamed the Dwight Correctional Center) in 1993. When the institution closed in 2013, most of its records went to the Illinois State Archives. But, at the time of this writing, the whereabouts of Eleanor's file/"jacket" remain unknown.

PART I. HARDSHIPS AND TEMPTATIONS
Chapter 1. Polka-Dotted Dress
This chapter drew largely from the same newspaper references as noted under chapter 16.

Chapter 2. The Tenth Child
The Woodbury County Courthouse in Sioux City, Iowa (via the Woodbury County Genealogical Society), forwarded documentation on Eleanor's birth, as well as the death of Eleanor's mother Amelia. Sioux City's Floyd Cemetery confirmed Amelia's burial, and the Sioux City Public Museum provided historic context.

The author accessed trees of other Ancestry.com members to learn of Eleanor's family relationships. Of great help (and also accessed via Ancestry.com) were federal census records, Iowa census records, Iowa birth (including delayed birth) records, Nebraska index to marriages, ship passenger lists, and Sioux City (Iowa) and Lincoln (Nebraska) city directories. Newspaper coverage included the *Lincoln Star* and the *Sioux City Journal*.

Chapter 3. Crimes
Chicago telephone books and city directories not available online were accessed through the Chicago History Museum. The museum also provided photographs from the *Chicago Sun-Times/Chicago Daily News* collection. Additional Chicago historical context can be accessed online at https://chicagology.com/. For context on fugitives of the era, the author viewed the film *I Am a Fugitive from a Chain Gang* (MGM/UAVintage

Classics, VHS tape, 1999 from the original 1932 film). Equally interesting context is found in Marianne Mather and Kori Rumore's book *He Had It Coming: Four Murderous Women and the Reporter Who Immortalized Their Stories* (Chicago Tribune, 2019).

Documentation of items stolen from the robbery victims were accessed through the Circuit Court of Cook County in *People vs. Eleanor Jarman et al*, 1933, specifically criminal cases CR-70150, CR-70151, CR-70152, CR-70153, CR-70154, and CR-70155. *Chicago Tribune* articles, however, inflated the values of some of the stolen items. On July 2, 1935, the Chicago Crime Commission summarized these cases.

Newspaper references included articles from the *Chicago Tribune*, *Democrat-News* (Fredericktown, Missouri), and the *Lincoln Star*. Selected newspaper and book references include:

- Allsop, Kenneth. *The Bootleggers and Their Era*. Doubleday, 1961.
- Staff. "Beer Flat Is New Method." *Daily Democrat-Forum and Maryville Tribune*, December 12, 1928.
- Staff. "Girl Helps in Robbery of Devon Avenue Store." *Chicago Tribune*, January 16, 1933.
- Staff. "Gunwoman's Visit Takes Ole Out of Circulation." Chicago Tribune, February 11, 1933.
- Staff. "Robberies Gain as Burglaries Drop in Chicago: Conviction Average on Increase." Chicago Tribune, May 8, 1933.

Chapter 4. Murder and Identification
This chapter relied heavily on Report #5160 from the Department of Police, City of Chicago. In addition to copies of original correspondence between the Chief Identification Inspector and the Captain of the 28th District, the report includes witness statements, the Coroner's Verdict, the Coroner's Verdict Card, and arrest records for Eleanor Jarman, George Kennedy (aka Dale), and Leo Minneci.

The Records of the Circuit Court of Cook County for *People vs. Eleanor Jarman et al*, 1933 included, as CR-70149, the defendants' indictments for murder. Leo Minneci's statement was excerpted from Supreme

Court of the State of Illinois, December Term A.D. 1933, *The People of the State of Illinois vs. George Dale, otherwise known as George Kennedy; Eleanor Jarman, and Leo Minneci.* In this same document, on pages 117–118, is a description of Hoeh's autopsy.

Selected newspaper references include:

- Gardner, Virginia. "Tiger Woman! Murder by Gun Girl and Two Companions; One of Trio Executed for Vicious Crime." *Chicago Tribune*, December 15, 1935.
- Staff. "Girl Leads Gang in Holdup; Aged Merchant Slain." *Chicago Tribune*, August 5, 1933.
- Staff. "Seize Member of Murder Gang; Mother of 2 Sought." *Chicago Tribune*, August 6, 1933.

Chapter 5. Cornered and Questioned

Eleanor Jarman's statement was excerpted from the Supreme Court of the State of Illinois, December Term A.D. 1933, *The People of the State of Illinois vs. George Dale, otherwise known as George Kennedy; Eleanor Jarman, and Leo Minneci.*

George Dale's statement was excerpted from a separate Illinois Supreme Court document titled *The People of the State of Illinois vs. George Dale, otherwise known as George Kennedy; Eleanor Jarman, and Leo Minneci; Brief and Argument for Plaintiff in Error*, also in the December 1933 term. John Dillinger was mentioned in this chapter. For more on him, see John Toland's *The Dillinger Days* (De Capo Press, 1995).

Selected newspaper references include:

- Staff. "Press Search for Woman in Holdup Murder; Scour W. Side for Blonde and Her Companion." *Chicago Tribune*, August 7, 1933.
- Staff. "Gunwoman Dyes Her Hair: Couple Seized for Merchant's Murder." *Lincoln Star Journal*, August 10, 1933.

- Staff. "Victims Identify 'Tiger Woman' in Score of Crimes; Point Out Gun Used to Kill Merchant." *Chicago Tribune*, August 11, 1933.

- Staff. "Blonde Tigress Is Identified by 37 Victims in All." *Chicago Tribune*, August 12, 1933.

- Staff. "'Blonde Tigress' Breaks Down in Police Show up." *Chicago Tribune*, August 14, 1933.

PART II. TRIAL

Chapter 6. Preliminary Proceedings

Chapter 6 draws from the records of the Circuit Court of Cook County in *People vs. Eleanor Jarman et al*, 1933, specifically CR-70149 (indictment for murder). Included is Christ Minneci's letter of August 21, 1933. The chapter also references the robbery cases (CR-70150–70155) and their summaries from the Chicago Crime Commission.

Selected newspaper references include:

- Staff. "Former Sioux Cityan Jailed; Mrs. Eleanor Jarman Is Held in Connection with a Murder." *Sioux City Journal*, August 13, 1933.

- Staff. "Former Sioux City Woman Is Held for Chicago Robberies." *Sioux City Journal*, August 15, 1933.

- Staff. "Speed Murder Trials of 7 in Crime War." *Chicago Tribune*, August 18, 1933.

- Staff. "Trial of Scheck, Police Killer, to Start Today: 'Blonde Tigress' and Two Pals to Face Court." *Chicago Tribune*, August 28, 1933.

Chapter 7. Trial, First Two Days

Again, this chapter draws from the records of the Circuit Court of Cook County in *People vs. Eleanor Jarman et al*, 1933, specifically CR-70149 (indictment for murder). Included is Eleanor's Petition for Change of Venue with the signed Affidavit of Richard Slater, as well as the petitions for a change of venue regarding judges and for severance. CR-70149 also includes the court's jury instructions.

Selected book and newspaper references include:

- Leonard, Lieutenant John D. *Police Manual*. Police Training School, 1936.
- Staff. "Says Electric Chair in Chicago Had Vacation Too Long." *Sioux City Journal*, August 19, 1933.
- Staff. "Trial of Scheck, Police Killer to Start Today; 'Blonde Tigress' and Two Pals to Face Court." *Chicago Tribune*, August 28, 1933.
- Staff. "'Tiger Girl' Faces Jury in Holdup Killing." *Chicago Tribune*, August 29, 1933.

Chapter 8. Trial, Prosecution

For background, procedure, and testimony in the defendants' trial, the author continued to rely on the Supreme Court of the State of Illinois, December Term A.D. 1933, *The People of the State of Illinois vs. George Dale, otherwise known as George Kennedy; Eleanor Jarman, and Leo Minneci*, archived at the Illinois State Archives, in Springfield, Illinois.

George Dale's petition, however, is excerpted from the second Supreme Court document—Supreme Court of the State of Illinois, December Term A.D. 1933, *The People of the State of Illinois vs. George Dale, otherwise known as George Kennedy; Eleanor Jarman, and Leo Minneci—Brief and Argument for Plaintiff in Error*.

Selected newspaper references include:

- Staff. "Four Accused of Murder, One a Woman, on Trial." *Chicago Tribune*, August 29, 1933.
- Staff. "State Closes Case Against 'Blonde Tigress' and Aids." *Chicago Tribune*, August 30, 1933.

Chapter 9. Trial, Defense

Again, the author continued to rely on the Supreme Court of the State of Illinois, December Term A.D. 1933, *The People of the State of Illinois vs. George Dale, otherwise known as George Kennedy; Eleanor Jarman, and Leo Minneci*, archived at the Illinois State Archives, in Springfield, Illinois.

Selected newspaper references include:

- Staff. "Give 'Tiger Girl' 199 Years." *Chicago Tribune*, August 31, 1933.
- Wright, George. "Sweetheart to Die in Chair for Holdup Murder." *Chicago Tribune*, August 31, 1933.
- Wright, George. "Record Term Fixed for 3d of Band." *Chicago Tribune*, August 31, 1933.

PART III. BEHIND BARS, 1933–1940

Chapter 10. One-Way Ticket

Much of this chapter is drawn from newspaper references. Selected ones include:

- Staff. "The Blonde Tigress." *Lincoln Star*, August 31, 1933.
- Staff. "Two Children of Convicted Killer Are Living Here." *Sioux City Journal*, September 1, 1933.
- Staff. "Life Sentence a Relief Says 'Tiger Woman'; Escape from Chair Brings Peaceful Sleep." *Chicago Tribune*, September 1, 1933.
- Staff. "Blonde Tigress Begins Trip to Prison Today: Her Pal Sentenced to Die Oct. 13." *Chicago Tribune*, September 2, 1933.
- Staff. "Blonde Tigress Leaves to Start Serving 199 Years in Prison." *Chicago Tribune*, September 3, 1933.
- Staff. "Tigress Weeps as Prison Door Closes on Her: 4 Other Women Begin to Pay for Crimes." *Chicago Tribune*, September 3, 1933.
- Staff. "Prisoners Arrive." *Dwight Star and Herald*, September 8, 1933.

Chapter 11. Oakdale Reformatory

Eleanor's intake forms (included in the "Petition for Commutation of Sentence on Behalf of Eleanor Jarman," from the Illinois Prisoner Review Board) were helpful in reconstructing Eleanor's personal information and the Oakdale Reformatory's entry protocol, despite some errors from the reformatory days. The "Dedication of Oakdale" program dates from November 19, 1931, at the time of the laying of the cornerstone of the Administration Building and clarifies the institution's founding and mission.

The *Trail Blazer* and articles from the *Dwight Star and Herald* were obtained from the Dwight Historical Society. In the section on Superintendent Helen H. Hazard, the author referenced the film *Women's Prison*, produced by Columbia Pictures in 1955. Selected newspaper and newsletter references include:

- Oakdale Reformatory Staff. *Trail Blazer: An Annual Number.* State Reformatory for Women, Dwight, Illinois, 1939.

- Several articles (some undated but circa 1929–1933) from the *Dwight Star and Herald* provided colorful context of the buildings and grounds.

- Six articles from December 1941 well describe the reformatory in its early years. All were published in *The Daily Pantagraph*, a newspaper from Bloomington, Illinois. Facts drawn from all of them are spread throughout the chapters in part III:

  - Campbell, Leonor. "Varied Personalities Make Up Population of Dwight Prison." *The Daily Pantagraph (Bloomington, Illinois)*, December 4, 1941.

  - Campbell, Leonor. "Killings, Stealings Are Main Causes for Imprisonments." *The Daily Pantagraph (Bloomington, Illinois)*, December 5, 1941.

  - Campbell, Leonor. "Kindness, Firmness Used in Rehabilitation of Prisoners." *The Daily Pantagraph (Bloomington, Illinois)*, December 6, 1941.

- Campbell, Leonor. "Inmates Taught How to be Good Workers." *The Daily Pantagraph (Bloomington, Illinois)*, December 7, 1941.

- Campbell, Leonor. "Rules Make Prisoner Aware She Is Not Free." *The Daily Pantagraph (Bloomington, Illinois)*, December 9, 1941.

- Campbell, Leonor. "Rehabilitation Big Task of Dwight Authorities." *The Daily Pantagraph (Bloomington, Illinois)*, December 11, 1941.

Chapter 12. A Room of Her Own

This chapter relied heavily on the *Pantagraph* articles, while Eleanor's early classification status was documented in the "Petition for Commutation of Sentence on Behalf of Eleanor Jarman," 1993. Selected newspaper references include:

- Staff. "Prison Inquiry Gives a Clean Bill to Dwight: Holds Women's Institution a Model One." *Chicago Tribune*, March 25, 1936.

- Staff. "Sioux Cityans to Aid Killer: Will Strive to Obtain New Trial for Eleanor Jarman." *Sioux City Journal*, September 7, 1933.

- Staff. "Chicago Courts Drive Back the Mountain Wave of Crime." *Chicago Tribune*, October 15, 1933.

Chapter 13. Supreme Court Appeal and George's Execution

Chapter 13 references the document titled *The People of the State of Illinois vs. George Dale, otherwise known as George Kennedy; Eleanor Jarman, and Leo Minneci—Brief and Argument for Plaintiff in Error*, by the Supreme Court of the State of Illinois, December Term A.D. 1933. Selected documents and newspaper references include:

- George Dale death certificate, number 11480, from Karen A. Yarbrough, Cook County Clerk, Chicago, Illinois.

- Leeds, Patricia. "The Blonde Tigress! Have You Seen Her? Vicious, Deadly, She'll Turn on the First Who Tries to Send Her

Back to Prison. She's the Most Dangerous Woman Alive!" *Chicago Tribune*, September 16, 1951.

- Nichols, Harman W. "'Nick' Witnesses Execution; Tells Story for Journal." *Farmer City Journal* (Farmer City, Illinois), April 26, 1934.
- Psychiatric Examination of George Dale, number 916, included in CR-70149 from the Circuit Court of Cook County.
- Staff. "Community Saddened Over Fate of George Dale Who Goes to the Electric Chair October 13." *Democrat-News (Fredericktown, Missouri)*, September 7, 1933.
- Staff. "John Dale to Chicago, Hoping to Save Son." *Democrat-News (Fredericktown, Missouri)*, September 21, 1933.
- Staff. "Governor Horner Refuses Clemency to George Dale: Slayer of Chicago Merchant to be Electrocuted April 20." *Associated Press*, April 14, 1934.
- Staff. "Two Slumber Before Going to Execution." *Chicago Tribune*, April 20, 1934.
- Staff. "Executed Slayer Buried." *Chicago Tribune*. April 24, 1934.
- Staff. "The Year the Electric Chair Claimed Its Last Victims in Illinois." *Chicago Tribune*, October 10, 1982.

Chapter 14. Eleanor Requests a Pardon

Of main importance in this chapter, and obtained from the Illinois State Archives, is the "Application for Commutation of Parole, Eleanor Jarman," filed with the Illinois Division of Pardons and Paroles on June 22, 1935. The application included Eleanor's "Petition for Commutation of Sentence," written by Parole Officer Martin M. Keegan. Included, too, are the letters of support from the following individuals:

- Mrs. Elsie Burrus
- Elmer K. Avery, M.D.
- Mrs. [Hermina] Goldschmidt

- Darrell Goldschmidt
- Mrs. Lula Herzfeld/Herzfield
- Mrs. Ollie Cox

Selected newspaper references include:

- Kelly, Frances M. "Life Fades Fast for Gangsters' Molls." *Los Angeles Times*, July 29, 1934.
- Staff. "Dwight Inmates Perform Most of Farm Work." *Chicago Tribune*, March 26, 1936.
- Staff. "Eleanor Jarman Pleads Commutation of Sentence." *Chicago Tribune*, July 10, 1935.
- Staff. "Horner Denies Clemency for Mrs. Hender." *The Belleville News-Democrat (in Belleville, Illinois)*, October 24, 1935.

Chapter 15. Margaret, a Fellow Felon

Margaret Keringer's (aka "Mary Foster's") "prison jacket," from Dwight Reformatory, 1940, was obtained from the Illinois State Archives. The author also corresponded with great-nephew Michael S. Makaron, who shared documents that were passed down through his family. Selected newspaper references include:

- Staff. "Went to Well Once Too Often." *Standard-Union (Brooklyn, New York)*, September 30, 1931.
- Staff. "Court Menace Puts Mackeron in Workhouse." *Standard-Union (Brooklyn, New York)*, December 12, 1931.
- Staff. "Demands a Home Before Quitting Prison for Hubby." *Daily News (New York, New York)*, August 25, 1933.
- Staff. "Girl Prisoner Escapes." *The Journal Times (Racine, Wisconsin)*, October 23, 1936.
- Staff. "Woman Bank Robber Sought." *Delaware County Daily Times (Chester, Pennsylvania)*, February 18, 1937.

- Staff. "Hunted by G-Men, Woman Gives Up; Fed After Sentence for Bank Holdup." *Detroit Free Press*, August 24, 1937.
- Staff. "Seize Housemaid As a Shoplifter, Find Bank Bandit." *Chicago Tribune*, December 24, 1938.

PART IV. MOST DANGEROUS WOMAN ALIVE
Chapter 16. August 1940

Federal census records (on Ancestry.com and FamilySearch.org) were researched to find personal information on Eleanor and her family members. The circa 1960 booklet "Look Toward the Future" by the Iowa State Institutions Board of Control provided context on the Iowa Training School for Boys in Eldora, Iowa. LeRoy Jarman's record with the Civilian Conservation Corps is outlined in his fourteen-page CCC Individual Record, Serial Number 7–317565, obtained from the National Personnel Records Center at the National Archives in St. Louis, Missouri. And the 1940 Chicago Telephone Directory (available from the Chicago History Museum) provided the address and telephone number for Richard Slater.

Selected book and newspaper references include:

- Clark, Jerry, and Ed Palattella. *On the Lam: A History of Hunting Fugitives in* America. Rowman & Littlefield, 2019.
- Lahey, Edwin A. "Good Night, Eleanor Jarman." *Chicago Daily News*, May 18, 1966.
- Staff. "Murderess Escapes." *The Daily Independent (Murphysboro, Illinois)*, August 8, 1940.
- Staff. "Hunt for 'Blonde Tigress' Turns Toward Joliet Area; Motorist Reports Picking Up Women Along Highway." *The Times* (Streator, Illinois), August 9, 1940.
- Staff. "Escapes." *The Daily Independent (Murphysboro, Illinois)*, August 9, 1940.
- Staff. "Hunt for Escaped Women Convicts Shifts to Joliet." *The Oshkosh Northwestern* (Oshkosh, Wisconsin), August 9, 1940.

- Staff. "Blond Tigress May Hide Here." *Sioux City Journal*, August 11, 1940.

Chapter 17. Means, Motive, and Opportunity

Although Richard Slater is referenced throughout this book, much of the research on him is concentrated in this chapter. The Slater sources include:

- Author's correspondence with Richard Slater's step-granddaughter, Sandra Oliver.
- Public records accessed through Ancestry.com and FamilySearch. org. that prove Richard Slater's family relationships with Hermina Goldschmidt, Darrell Goldschmidt, Lula Herzfeld/Herzfield, and Ollie Cox.
- Hermina Goldschmidt, Darrell Goldschmidt, Lula Herzfeld/Herzfield, and Ollie Cox's letters of support are contained in Eleanor Jarman's "Application for Commutation of Parole, 1935." Illinois State Archives.
- Eleanor Jarman's mention of Slater on page 159 of Supreme Court of the State of Illinois, December Term A.D. 1933, *The People of the State of Illinois vs. George Dale, otherwise known as George Kennedy; Eleanor Jarman, and Leo Minneci*. Illinois State Archives.
- Eleanor Jarman's Petition for Change of Venue with the signed Affidavit of Richard Slater in *People vs. Eleanor Jarman et al*, 1933, CR-70149 (indictment for murder). Circuit Court of Cook County.
- Richard Slater's World War II Selective Service card, 1942. National Archives at St. Louis, Missouri.
- Lake County, Illinois, Clerk's Office for its Grantor Index 1936–1957, and related property records.

Selected newspaper references include:

- Gardner, Virginia. "Tiger Woman! Murder by Gun Girl and Two Companions; One of Trio Executed for Vicious Crime." *Chicago Tribune*, December 15, 1935.

- Staff. "In Zuta Box; Gang Payments Listed to Public Officials." *Chicago Tribune*, August 16, 1930.

- Staff. "Circle Village in Hunt for Pal of 'Tiger Girl.'" *Chicago Tribune*, August 10, 1940.

- Staff. "Zuta's Records Reveal Kalb as Gaming Partner: Worked Together in the Northwest Sections." *Chicago Tribune*, August 25, 1930.

Chapter 18. Ordinary Woman or "Blonde Tigress"?

This chapter referenced a copy of the SS-5 Form (from the Social Security Administration) for the alias of Twylia May Embrey, as noted in the author's book *Someone's Daughter: In Search of Justice for Jane Doe* (Taylor Trade, 2009; and updated edition, Lyons Press, 2023). The author also filed a Freedom of Information Act (FOIA) Request with the Federal Bureau of Investigation regarding the files of Eleanor Jarman, FBI #2072992, with letters regarding possible "sightings." In addition, the 1950s television show *Gang Busters* (Series 1, Episode 10, "The Blonde Tigress") epitomized the media's fixation on sensationalism at this time.

Selected newspaper and magazine references include:

- Campbell, Leonor. "Rehabilitation Big Task of Dwight Authorities." *The Daily Pantagraph (Bloomington, Illinois)*, December 11, 1941.

- Enstad, Robert. "Active in Law at 80; Wants 10 More Years." *Chicago Tribune*, January 3, 1965.

- Finger Print Publishing Association. *Finger Print and Identification Magazine*. Chicago: Volume 24, Number 10, April 1943.

- Mundis, James M. "Where Is the Blonde Tigress?" *Front Page Detective Magazine*, Volume 11, Number 7, November 1947.

- O'Brien, John. "53 Years on the Run—Family Seeks Clemency for 'Blonde Tigress' in '33 Chicago Murder." *Chicago Tribune*, July 11, 1993.

- Staff. "Captured Gun Girl Expresses Regret Pistol Not Loaded." *Muncie Evening Press (Muncie, Indiana)*, May 24, 1950.

- Woltman, George. "70 Flee Dwight Prison in 23 Years; 4 Still at Large." *Chicago Tribune*, October 18, 1953.

Chapter 19. Lost in Time

Again, as in chapter 15, the author corresponded with Margaret Keringer's grand-nephew Michael S. Makaron, who shared his documents on Margaret. Biographical data on Margaret Keringer, as well as Michael Roy Jarman, was obtained via Ancestry.com and FamilySearch.org. Additional information on Richard Slater came from continued correspondence with his step-granddaughter, as well as genealogical websites. The following documents were accessed in researching the Jarman family's request for clemency:

- 1993 Petition and Amended Petition for Commutation of Sentence, Eleanor Jarman, obtained from the Illinois Prisoner Review Board.

- Prisoner Review Board chairman's correspondence with Attorney David P. Schippers, obtained from the Illinois Prisoner Review Board.

Selected newspaper, magazine, and poster references include:

- Brakefield, Jay. "Fugitive Tales: Fueled by Hollywood Magic or Real-life Drama, Stories of People on the Run Capture Our Interest." *Dallas Morning News*, August 29, 1993.

- Federal Bureau of Investigation, Eleanor Jarman Wanted poster, FBI #2072992, obtained from the FBI and in the public domain.

- O'Brien, John. "Clemency Lawyer Asks Fugitive to Contact Him." *Chicago Tribune*, June 30, 1993.

- O'Brien, John. "53 Years on the Run—Family Seeks Clemency for 'Blonde Tigress' in '33 Chicago Murder." *Chicago Tribune*, July 11, 1993.

- O'Brien, John. "Clemency Board Denies Hearing for Fugitive Who Escaped in '40." *Chicago Tribune*, October 7, 1993.

- O'Brien, John. "Hunt for 'Blond Tigress' Nearing End for Grandson." *Chicago Tribune*, December 11, 1994.

- Pollock, Jim. "Iowan Searches for 'The Blonde Tigress.'" *Des Moines Register*, March 9, 1994.

- Staff. "Police Seize 34 in Gaming Raid on V.F.W. Club." *Chicago Tribune*, November 25, 1949.

- Staff. "Fugitives From the FBI: Eleanor Jarman." *King Features Syndicate*, April 30, 1953.

- Staff. "TD Line-Up: Watch for These Fugitives." *True Detective* Magazine, Volume 61, Number 2, June 1954.

- Staff. "Fugitive Warrant for Woman Slayer Dropped on Request." *Chicago Tribune*, November 22, 1954.

- Staff. "Cut Sentence of Murderer." *The Times (Hammond, Indiana)*, August 16, 1957.

- Staff. "Family of 'Most Dangerous' Woman Tries to Clear Her Name." *Associated Press*, June 29, 1993.

- Thompson, Kate. "Where Is the 'Blonde Tigress?'" *Sioux City Journal*, June 11, 1994.

- Thompson, Kate. "Grandson of 1940 Escapee Reveals Name She Used." *Sioux City Journal*, December 11, 1994.

- Varga, Lou. "True Family Celebration: Brothers, Sisters are Reunited After 37 Years of Separation." *The Signal (Santa Clarita, California)*, April 18, 1989.

Chapter 20. Tables Turned

The search for Eleanor's alias, Marie Millman, involved the following sources:

- The author searched genealogical databases Ancestry.com and FamilySearch.org for any family members. There were none. Denver City Directories, however, provided a list of addresses for Eleanor's alias, Marie Millman. On Ancestry.com, the author created a private "Marie Millman Research Tree." There were *no* family members. At the time of this writing, the tree has been online for more than a year, and there have been *no* "hints."

- A "Request for Earnings Record for Marie H. Millman" was obtained from the Social Security Administration. The agency could *not* provide any other information.

- A Freedom of Information/Privacy Act (FOIPA) request on Marie Millman stated that, in the FBI's records, Marie had *no* paper trail.

- The Denver Probate Court's "Petition for Final Settlement and Distribution in the Matter of the Estate of Marie Millman, Probate Number 80-PR-1207" showed *no* heirs.

- Fairmount Cemetery records, including a map of Fairmount Cemetery, Denver Colorado, records Marie Millman's burial in Section 5, Lot 540, Block 67.

Selected additional references include:

- Historic Denver Guide "East Colfax Avenue" on the website of the Denver Public Library, Denver, Colorado.

- Lahey, Edwin A. "Good Night, Eleanor Jarman." *Chicago Daily News*, May 18, 1966.

- Staff. "Funeral records, Capitol Mortuary, Marie Millman." *Denver Post*, August 18, 1980.

- Staff. "New Clues Indicate 'Blond Tigress' Trail Might Not Be Cold." *Chicago Tribune*, December 26, 1994.

INDEX